T0023652

As Richard Belcher explains in the opening of this book, covenant theology is the Bible's operating system. It provides a unified framework for understanding how God relates to us and how we relate to God. But, like many operating systems, grasping the details of covenant theology can be challenging. Thankfully, Dr. Belcher has written an introductory guide that defines technical terms like "cutting a covenant," unpacks complicated ideas like the covenant of works, and shows how the various biblical covenants in Scripture hang together in relation to the person and work of Jesus Christ. Well-researched and concisely written, Richard Belcher's Christ Fulfills All will be the first resource I recommend to anyone wanting to learn more about covenant theology.

JOHN W. TWEEDDALE
Vice President of Academics and Professor of Theology,
Reformation Bible College, Sanford, Florida

An outstanding introduction to covenant theology as set forth in the Westminster Standards. If you are new to covenant theology, or if you are looking for resources to help others understand this vital topic in biblical studies, this book is for you. It is clear, concise, and accessible. Belcher's academic experience combined with his pastoral sensitivity are evident throughout.

MILES V. VAN PELT
Professor of Old Testament and Biblical Languages,
Reformed Theological Seminary, Jackson, Mississippi

This short book is a superb introduction to covenant theology. For anyone seeking to understand how God's covenant promises run through all the pages of Scripture, and for anyone seeking to marvel anew at how Christ fulfills them all, this book is the first place to go.

THOMAS DAVIS
Minister, Carloway Free Church of Scotland, Isle of Lewis,
author, *God is God and You are You*

Belcher expertly weaves together a portrait of the biblical-theological landscape of how God has covenanted with his people into an amazingly accessible little book. This work should be a first port of call for those new to covenant theology. Belcher's user-friendly style and irenic tone lead us into more depth than we might expect from a book so easy to read.

HARRISON PERKINS
Pastor, Oakland Hills Community Church (OPC),
Farmington Hills, Michigan;
author, *A Student's Guide to Living Out Reformed Theology*

CHRIST FULFILLS ALL
INTRODUCING THE BIBLICAL COVENANTS

RICHARD P. BELCHER, JR.

CHRISTIAN
FOCUS

paperback ISBN 978-1-5271-1134-9
ebook ISBN 978-1-5271-1181-3

10 9 8 7 6 5 4 3 2 1

Published in 2024

by

Christian Focus Publications Ltd.,
Geanies House, Fearn, Ross-shire
IV20 1TW, Great Britain.

www.christianfocus.com

Cover design by Rubner Durais

Printed and bound by
Bell and Bain Glasgow

Contents

Preface

Why Study Covenant Theology?

There are some things in life that make other things possible. When I use my computer or cell phone, I only worry about what I need to know to operate them. I have very little understanding of the operating systems that run my electronic devices. I do not need to know how the system runs because, if I have problems, I know where to find help. I can get by without knowing the complexities of what runs my computer or cell phone. Many times, we are dependent on things that we do not really understand. On the other hand, if we are going to learn a language, there are grammatical rules that we need to know. For example, the normal English word order is subject, verb, and then object, but that is not the order followed by every language. The better you understand the rules of grammar for a language the better you will be able to speak, write, or read it. We learn the language of our childhood by being immersed in it without always knowing the specific grammatical rules for it. I teach students to read ancient Hebrew so they can read the Old Testament in the original language. They learn (or relearn) many grammatical principles so they can understand Hebrew. The better the students know Hebrew grammar, the better they will be able to understand Hebrew.

Many Christians have read their Bibles all their lives. They understand many things about the Bible. But the Bible is a complex book. It has sixty-six different books with many different authors composed over a 1,500-year period. It is difficult to grasp the make up and message of such a diverse book. Covenant theology will help you better understand the Bible because it gives structure to the whole Bible, and it is the language in which the Bible is written. The more you understand the structure of the Bible the better you will understand the major message of the Bible and see how everything fits together. There is a unity to the message of the Bible centered around covenant theology related to God's plan to restore broken human beings who have rebelled against him. Covenant theology explains how we became broken and how God plans to save us.

Covenant theology is a pervasive concept that occurs all throughout Scripture. The more one understands it, the more one will understand the language of Scripture. The Bible uses many ideas that are better understood in the context of covenant theology. The following ideas are related to it even if people might not see the connection at first: Old Testament/New Testament, the blood of the covenant sprinkled on the people followed by a meal (Exod. 24:6, 11), mediators, laws, blessings and curses, the statement 'this cup is the new covenant in my blood' (Lord's Supper), God's promise 'I will be their God and they will be

---

Point of Interest

Although the Bible was written by many human authors over a long period of time, the ultimate author of the Bible is God, who worked with the personalities and gifts of the various human authors to produce the very words of Scripture (2 Tim. 3:16–17; 2 Pet. 1:20–21). Because the Bible ultimately has one divine author, there is unity to the message of the whole Bible.

my people,' and God's dwelling with his people are just a few of the many concepts that are better understood in the context of covenant theology. As will become clear, the gospel itself is dependent on the covenantal framework of Scripture. The covenants explain the work of Christ and the covenant signs of baptism and the Lord's Supper. Covenants also give assurance to God's people because we see that God is faithful to his covenant promises. We can be confident that our relationship with God is secure.

In summary, the main benefit of covenant theology is that it will help you understand the Bible better. You will be able to see connections between different parts of the Bible and understand how the OT lays the foundation of the NT. You will come to see the great unity to God's plan of redemption and how God is working out that plan in history. No longer will the OT be just a series of unconnected stories or miscellaneous parts. Abraham and Moses and David, along with many others, all have their role to play in the unfolding of God's purposes that will be fulfilled in Jesus Christ.

The goal of this brief book is to explain covenant theology as it is expressed in the Westminster Standards (the Westminster Confession of Faith and the Larger and Shorter Catechisms).* This Confession was produced at the Westminster Assembly in 1646 as an attempt to reform the structures, worship, and teaching of the church. It is a summary of Christian theology in

---

* Throughout the rest of this book, the Westminster Confession of Faith will be abbreviated WCF, the Westminster Larger Catechism WLC, and the Westminster Shorter Catechism WSC. This pocket guide has a limited number of footnotes. For a more in-depth discussion of covenant theology with full documentation see Richard P. Belcher, Jr., *The Fulfillment of the Promises of God: An Explanation of Covenant Theology* (Ross-shire: Christian Focus, 2020). For a more comprehensive analysis of covenant theology see *Covenant Theology: Biblical, Theological, and Historical Perspectives*, eds. Guy P. Waters, J. Nicholas Reid, and John R. Muether (Crossway, 2020). There is also a list of Suggested Reading at the end of the book that includes a wide variety of views of covenant theology.

the Reformation tradition. The doctrine of the covenant is one of its distinctive features because the covenant is central to its system of theology. It was the first confessional standard to use the terms Covenant of Works and Covenant of Grace. It greatly affected the churches of England, Wales, Scotland, and Ireland. It was also adopted by conservative Presbyterian denominations all over the world. One of the purposes of this pocket guide is to engage seminary students and elders but specially to help lay people understand covenant theology. Even if you are not part of a denomination that subscribes to the WCF, understanding its view of covenant will give you a foundation to understand the basic concepts of covenant theology and help you see where you might differ. The next chapter will define a covenant, then the overall structure of covenant theology in Scripture will be laid out before examining each of the major covenants and how they are fulfilled in the new covenant.

Point of Interest

Some of the Presbyterian denominations that have adopted the Westminster Standards in the U.S.A. include the Associate Reformed Presbyterian Church, the Orthodox Presbyterian Church, the Presbyterian Church in America, and the Evangelical Presbyterian Church. Many other Presbyterian denominations around the world have also adopted it, including the Free Church of Scotland, the International Presbyterian Church, the Evangelical Presbyterian Church of England and Wales, the Presbyterian Church of Australia, the Presbyterian Church of Brazil, and the National Presbyterian Church in Mexico, among others. Some Baptists have adopted the Second London Confession of 1689, which is like the WCF but with Baptist distinctives. There are other denominations, such as the Presbyterian Church in the United States of America, that formally adopted the Westminster Standards but don't functionally adhere to them.

1

What Is a Covenant?

Most of us are familiar with a contract. It is a formal and legally binding agreement between two or more parties that sets forth the responsibilities that each party is obligated by law to fulfill. It is usually a written document signed by all the parties involved. Contracts usually deal with financial agreements, business agreements, employment agreements, and rental agreements. A breach of contract can be very serious because there are legal consequences for breaking it. A covenant is like a contract because they both structure relationships that have a legal aspect to them that bind the parties to the terms of the agreement with consequences if either party fails to fulfill their obligations.

DIFFERENT ASPECTS OF A COVENANT RELATIONSHIP

A covenant is also very different from a contract. A covenant has broader implications because the legal aspect is tied to personal and corporate aspects that are typically not present in contracts. When I sign a loan agreement with a bank, I normally do not personally know the people with whom I am dealing. The contract normally deals only with me and my spouse unless it is a situation where a cosigner is involved. A covenant is much broader. There are personal and corporate aspects of a covenant that affect the legal aspect of the covenant. These three aspects of a covenant are intertwined and operate together.

Marriage is a good example of how a covenant works. There is a legal aspect to a marriage that is expressed in the promises (vows) the couple make to each other. There is also a ring that is exchanged that acts as a sign pointing to the existence of the promises that were made. It is a binding relationship that lasts until death and there are legal consequences if one party breaks the promises. There is also a personal relationship in marriage where the couple express their love for each other. Sadly, many times the love between a couple may diminish because of difficulties in the relationship. It is possible for there to be a legal marriage between two people even though they are no longer in love with each other. Couples may decide to stay legally married even though they are no longer in love for a variety of reasons (finances, children, appearances). Finally, there are corporate dimensions to a marriage covenant. Marriage does not just involve the union of two individuals, but each spouse also must navigate the relationships with the in-laws and the prospect of children that might develop from the marriage. A marriage covenant that has legal, personal, and corporate aspects is much broader than a contract.

The covenants in the Bible, especially the covenants that God makes with his people, also have legal, personal, and corporate aspects to them. God makes a covenant to establish personal relationships with his people. He would regularly come down to the Garden of Eden to have fellowship with Adam and Eve. Their disobedience to God's command broke the personal relationship that had been established and then he came into the garden in judgment to confront them for their rebellion (Gen. 3:8). In his grace, God provided a way to restore the broken relationship through a series of covenants that culminated in the New Covenant. God initiated this covenant with Adam after his disobedience in Genesis 3, then he established a covenant with Noah, Abraham, Israel as mediated through Moses, David, and finally the New Covenant in Christ. The essence of this covenant relationship is expressed in the recurring phrase, 'I shall be your God and you shall be my people.' This phrase, or something very similar to it, is found in each of the covenants: Genesis 17:7 (Abraham); Exodus 6:6–7 (Israel); 2 Kings 11:17 (Davidic); Ezekiel 37:26–28 (promise of the New Covenant), and Revelation 21:3 (consummation of the New Covenant). The promise of a relationship with God is manifested in God's dwelling amid his people in the tabernacle (Exod. 25:8; 29:42–45), then the temple (1 Kings 8:10), culminating in Jesus Christ as God with us (John 1:14). God desires to dwell with his people in a gracious relationship of fellowship.*

The corporate aspect of the covenant has several angles to it. At the heart of a covenant relationship is the representative principle. The disobedience of Adam affected not only himself, but also all his descendants because he was their representative acting on their behalf. We see the consequences of his sin in his life (Gen. 3) and in the lives of his sons (Gen. 4). In the various covenants in the Old Testament, God will use an individual to begin the covenant relationship so that the promises and terms of the covenant can be stated. This explains why many of the covenants are called by the name of the person with whom God established the covenant (Noah, Abraham, Moses, David). Another corporate aspect of the covenant is that all the covenants include the descendants of the person with whom

---

* O. Palmer Robertson, *The Christ of the Covenants* (P&R Publishing, 1980), pp. 46–51. For an emphasis on the theme of God dwelling with his people see Michael L. Morales, *Who Shall Ascend the Mountain of the Lord? A biblical theology of the book of Leviticus* (InterVarsity Press, 2015).

God makes the covenant. Not only did Adam's disobedience affect his descendants, but the enmity of Genesis 3:15 will be worked out through the descendants of the seed of the woman and the seed of the serpent. This will culminate in a final representative who will defeat Satan and win the victory for the seed of the woman. The corporate principle will be discussed in each of the covenants to see how the covenant promises affect the descendants, who are always included in the terms of the covenant. All the promises will culminate in Jesus Christ, our representative, who fulfills the covenant promises in his life and death as he establishes the New Covenant.

Finally, there is a legal aspect to the covenant relationship that is foundational to the administration of the covenant. This aspect can include oaths and rituals, like sacrifices, that confirm the covenant relationship and make clear the terms of the relationship. How is the covenant administered? How is it passed on to future generations? What consequences are there if the terms of the covenant are broken? The ideal is that the legal, personal, and corporate aspects of the covenant work together to bring about a harmonious relationship between God and his people. The presence of disobedience breaks the covenant and results in covenant judgment where some members of the covenant may be cut off from the blessings of the covenant. This means that not everyone who is a member of the covenant has a saving relationship with the God of the covenant. Christ brings together the legal, personal, and corporate aspects of the covenant in the New Covenant, which will have implications for how we understand the nature and function of his body, the church, in this age and in the age to come.

DEFINITION AND ELEMENTS OF A COVENANT

A covenant can be defined as a legal agreement between two parties that is ratified by oaths and certain rituals that stress the binding nature of the agreement. The phrase that is used to make a covenant in the Old Testament is 'to cut a covenant.' The idea of cutting highlights the rituals of sacrifices and oaths that are at the heart of a covenant relationship (Gen. 15:7–18). Covenants are made in a variety of situations. There are covenants between human parties who are equal (Gen. 21:27, 26:26–31, 31:44–55; 1 Sam. 8:13), between human parties who are not equal (Josh. 9:3–21; 1 Sam. 11:1; 1 Kings 20:34), and between God and humans (Gen. 6:18, 15:18, 17:2; Exod. 19:5; 2 Sam. 7; Ps. 89:3). Of course, God is always the superior party in any relationship.

Common elements in covenants include promises made and oaths taken to ensure the promises will be carried out. There are stipulations or laws that must be kept. Blessings are promised if the covenant is kept, but curses are threatened if the covenant is broken. Covenants include descendants and are generally ratified by blood. Not every mention of covenant in Scripture includes the rituals

> ## Point of Interest
>
> When one nation conquered another nation a covenant was established between the nations. The conquering king (called the suzerain) entered a covenant with the conquered king and nation (called the vassal). This type of covenant was called a Treaty and the laws of this covenant regulated the relationship between the parties and included benefits if the laws were obeyed and negative consequences (curses) if the laws were disobeyed. Many argue that the book of Deuteronomy fits the treaty type of covenant.[*]
>
> ---
>
> [*] Meredith Kline, *Treaty of the Great King: The Covenant Structure of Deuteronomy* (Wipf and Stock, 2012).

that establish the covenant, but the importance of sacrifices is seen in the covenant with Abraham (Gen. 15:7–18). Many times, witnesses are a testimony to the covenant that has been ratified (Gen. 31:44–47). The importance of stipulations (laws) and sanctions (penalties for breaking the covenant) are seen in the covenant with Moses (Lev. 26; Deut. 27–28). Covenants also produced written documents where the promises, stipulations, and sanctions are spelled out, as in Deuteronomy. Finally, signs are important in covenants, such as the rainbow (Gen. 9:12–13), circumcision (Gen. 17:11), and the Sabbath (Exod. 31:16–17).

Point of Interest

The covenants of the ancient Near East called the gods as witnesses when the covenant was made, but if the Bible mentions witnesses to the agreements established in the covenant, creation itself served as a witness (Isa. 1:2).

2

The Covenantal Structure of Scripture

Covenant is a central concept in Scripture that will help you understand many passages and ideas as you read through the Bible. But even more, covenants give structure to Scripture that help you see how all the different parts of Scripture fit together. In this way, covenants give unity to Scripture and help us see the outworking of God's plan of redemption from Genesis through Revelation. Covenants are like an iceberg. Sometimes they are very visible because the Bible explains the role of different covenants. But many times, the effects of a covenant are operative without the covenant being clearly seen, like the part of the iceberg that is underwater. Covenantal structure has also been compared to a house. The internal structure of a house that cannot be seen, including load-bearing walls and beams, gives a house stability and allows many of the adornments of the house to be visible. Covenants give structure to God's redemptive plan, but they also provide some of the adornment of the house that we can see clearly. The purpose of this chapter is to lay out the role that covenants play in giving structure to Scripture. The following chapters will explain the individual covenants, how they relate to each other, and how they are fulfilled in the New Covenant.

THE COVENANT OF REDEMPTION

Reformed theology typically speaks of three major covenants: the Covenant of Redemption, the Covenant of Works, and the Covenant of Grace. These three covenants give structural unity to God's plan of redemption. The Covenant of Redemption, also called the Counsel of Peace (*pactum salutis*), is a covenant made before time began between the persons of the Trinity to ensure that the divine plan of redemption would be carried out in history. The word 'covenant' is not used in Scripture to describe this agreement, but there is scriptural evidence of this divine plan to ensure the salvation of God's people. Ephesians 1 lays out the role of each person of the Trinity: the Father has chosen us in Christ before the foundation of the world and has predestined us for adoption as sons through Jesus Christ (1:3–5); the Son redeemed us through his blood that we might receive the forgiveness of our sins and the inheritance that he has purchased for us (1:7–11); the Holy Spirit applies the work of Christ to our lives and helps us persevere until the day that we receive our full inheritance in glory (1:13–14).

The biblical basis for the Covenant of Redemption is found in the way Jesus talks about his relationship to the Father. First, the Father sent Jesus on a mission giving him works to accomplish (John 5:36–37; 17:4). Jesus does not do his own will but the will of the Father who sent him (John 6:38; 12:49). Jesus has been given a charge by the Father to lay down his life (John 10:18). Second, the Father has given to the Son a group of people that he will redeem. They will come to him, and he will not lose any of them but will raise them up on the last day (6:37–40). Third, the relation between the Father and the Son is conditioned on the obedience of the Son with the promise of a reward. Christ has kept the Father's commandments and abides in his love (John 15:10). Christ asks the Father to glorify him with the glory he had before the world existed because he has accomplished the work the Father gave him to do (John 17:4–5). Christ is exalted to the right hand of the Father because he was obedient unto death (Phil. 2:8–9).* The work of the Spirit applies the redemption that Christ has accomplished. Jesus tells his disciples that the Spirit that he would send would preserve them (John 15:26–16:4) and purify them (John 14:17, 21–24) through the truth and love of God (John 14:15–18, 26). The Son's reward from the Father will be realized through the Spirit. Jesus' high priestly prayer in John 17 asks that the ones given to him by the Father would be preserved (17:11–12) and purified (17:19) with eternal truth and divine love (17:17, 25–26) to help them amid the opposition they will face (17:15–19).

Point of Interest

Not everyone agrees that there is a Covenant of Redemption. Many evangelical scholars and some Reformed theologians deny the existence of the Covenant of Redemption. They might recognize the role of redemption in the eternal counsels of God or that there is an agreement between the members of the Trinity to work out our salvation, but they do not want to call it a covenant. In fact, many early reformed Confessions, such as the Belgic Confession, the Heidelberg Catechism, the Canons of Dordt, and the WCF did not explicitly refer to the Covenant of Redemption, but they contained ideas that were foundational for understanding it.* Many of the delegates who participated in the Westminster Assembly that produced the WCF affirmed it. Ideas that would support the Covenant of Redemption are expressed in comments concerning Christ fulfilling the stipulations of the covenant as the mediator of his people (WCF 8).

---

* David Van Drunen and R. Scott Clark, 'The Covenants before the Covenants,' in *Covenant, Justification, and Pastoral Ministry*, ed. R. Scott Clark (P&R, 2007), pp. 167–96.

---

* For more biblical and theological justification of the Covenant of Redemption see Guy M. Richard, 'The Covenant of Redemption,' in *Covenant Theology*, eds. Guy P. Waters, et al., pp. 43–62.

THE COVENANT OF WORKS

The Covenant of Redemption is the backbone of both the Covenant of Works and the Covenant of Grace. The Covenant of Works is the mirror image of the Covenant of Redemption. There is no mediator in either covenant. The Covenant of Redemption is made between God the Father and God the Son and the Covenant of Works is made between God the Father and Adam, who is called the Son of God (Luke 3:38). Just as Adam was tempted, so was the second Adam. The failure of Adam did not catch God by surprise but was part of his plan from the foundation of the world. God the Son would need to come into the world to succeed where Adam failed. These connections show that there is a covenant between God and Adam that failed because of Adam's disobedience and that there is also a covenant between the members of the Trinity to carry out the plan that failed when Adam disobeyed God. When Christ kept the law, he was fulfilling both the historical Covenant of Works made with Adam and the pretemporal Covenant of Redemption he made with the Father and the Spirit.

The evidence for a Covenant of Works will be presented in a future chapter so here only a summary will be given related to the differences between the Covenant of Works and the Covenant of Grace. God created Adam, gave him a job to do, and equipped him to do that job. Adam represented not only himself, but he also acted as a representative for all his descendants so that his actions would affect them. God also gave Adam a specific law related to the trees that were in the garden. God commanded Adam saying, 'You may surely eat of every tree of the garden, but of the tree of the knowledge of good and evil you shall not eat, for in the day you eat of it you shall surely die' (Gen. 2:16–17).

This command is a specific test that God gave to Adam. It is a negative command that even though there are an abundance of trees in the garden from which Adam may eat, there is one tree from which he may not eat. If Adam disobeys this command, the penalty is death. Adam had the ability to keep this command, but he was also able to disobey it. God gave Adam a test that focused on one command related to one tree. This test represented God's requirement for personal and perpetual obedience. If disobedience brought death, it follows that if Adam obeyed the command, the reward would be an advancement of Adam's life. The tree of life was also in the garden and confirmed that the reward was related to life. If Adam had obeyed God and had passed this test, he would have advanced to a state of eternal life, a life where he would not be able to sin.

The probationary test that God gave to Adam was at the heart of the Covenant of Works. Although there was a personal relationship between God and Adam, there was also a legal relationship. If Adam had obeyed God, he could have procured for himself and his posterity the benefits of obedience. Sin would not have entered the world. But Adam failed the test and plunged himself and his posterity into sin and its effects. The fellowship they had with God in the garden was lost. Every descendant of Adam is born with a sinful nature and therefore tainted with sin, but the obligation to keep God's law perfectly is still a requirement for every human being. The problem is we are not able to keep God's law and so we are condemned by that law. The only hope of salvation and for renewed fellowship with God is for a second Adam to fully obey the law on our behalf. The basis for a second Adam is promised and then fulfilled in the Covenant of Grace.

THE COVENANT OF GRACE

The Covenant of Grace is very different from the Covenant of Works. In the Covenant of Works God showed kindness and goodwill toward Adam by providing all that he needed to live in the garden and to fulfill the mandate God had given him to do. Once Adam disobeyed God, sin entered the picture and God began to treat Adam with redemptive grace, which can be defined as favor toward someone who does not deserve it. Although Adam experienced the negative consequences of his disobedience, he also experienced God's undeserved grace in many ways (see the chapter on 'The Initiation of the Covenant of Grace'). It is important to distinguish the different ways God related to Adam in the Covenant of Works before the Fall and the Covenant of Grace after the Fall. The technical term for these two covenants is bi-covenantal. When people argue that God related to Adam the same way before and after the Fall in one covenant (mono-covenantal), there is a tendency to downplay the legal aspects of the Covenant of Works, which can affect one's view of justification by faith and the imputation of Christ's righteousness to us.

God responded to Adam's sin with grace. Even though sin brought negative consequences and destroyed God's fellowship with Adam and Eve, God acted with grace to negate some of those consequences, and he promised to restore fallen humanity through his plan of redemption. The Covenant of Grace is initiated in the garden with Adam and was worked out in a variety of covenants in the rest of the OT, namely, the covenants with Noah, Abraham, Moses, and David. These OT covenants culminated in the New Covenant brought about by the person and work of Christ. Each of these covenants will be discussed in the following chapters.

The Covenant of Grace is based upon the Covenant of Redemption because salvation is applied to the elect based on the work of Christ. The Covenant of Grace is enacted in time which implies that there must be another covenant before the beginning of time in which the conditions and the promises of the Covenant of Grace are established. Hebrews 7:20–22 speaks of the oath between the Father and the Son. Also, Christ functions as a mediator of the Covenant of Grace which means that this covenant was enacted with him personally (Ps. 2; Luke 22:29; and Heb. 7). The Covenant of Redemption establishes and guarantees the Covenant of Grace by establishing and guaranteeing Christ's role in it.[*] Based on this relationship, it is appropriate to understand the Covenant of Grace as one covenant worked out in history. As stated in WCF 7.5,

> This covenant was differently administered in the time of the law, and in the time of the gospel: under the law it was administered by promises, prophecies, sacrifices, circumcision, the paschal lamb, and other types of ordinances, delivered to the people of the Jews, all foresignifying Christ to come.

The next section (WCF 7.6) states that 'There are not therefore two covenants of grace, differing in substance, but one and the same, under various dispensations.' The word 'dispensations' refers to the various administrations of the covenant. Although the covenants of the Old Testament are different in how they are administered (see WCF 7.5), there is a substantial unity between the covenants of the Old Testament and the New Covenant. We will see how this works out in our discussions of each of the Old Testament covenants.

---

[*] Guy M. Richard, 'The Covenant of Redemption,' in *Covenant Theology,* eds Guy P. Waters, et al., pp. 58–59.

3

The Covenant of Works

The Covenant of Works is a foundational covenant in Scripture that has implications for the gospel. The work of Christ, including his obedience, his relationship with Adam, and his role as a mediator are all related to the Covenant of Works. These doctrines are also important for justification by faith.

THE EVIDENCE FOR A COVENANT OF WORKS

The word 'covenant' does not occur in Scripture until the flood account in Genesis 6:18. If the word 'covenant' does not occur in Genesis 1–3, why should we think there is a covenant established between God and Adam? The absence of the word 'covenant' does not necessarily mean that there is not a covenant in Genesis 1–3. The word 'covenant' does not occur in 2 Samuel 7 or 1 Chronicles 17 where God makes certain promises to David, but other passages refer to this relationship as a covenant (2 Sam. 23:5; Ps. 89:3, 28; 132:11–12). A similar situation occurs with Genesis 1–3. The term covenant is not used in the early chapters of Genesis, but later Scripture refers to Genesis 1–3 and uses the term 'covenant.' The key is not whether the term 'covenant' occurs in Genesis 1–3 but whether the elements of a covenant are present.

The Elements of a Covenant in Genesis 1–3

Several elements commonly associated with covenants are present in Genesis 1–3. First, the parties to the covenant are clearly identified. Genesis 1:1 assumes the existence of God who is 'in the beginning.' He is the sovereign ruler of the universe as demonstrated in his creation of the world. Special attention is given to his creation of mankind in his image who have a special place in creation under his authority (Gen. 1:26–28). In Genesis 1, the general term for humanity is used (*adam*); in Genesis 2, the specific partners in this covenant are identified as Adam (*adam*) and Eve. God takes the initiative in creating the world and in entering a covenant relationship with the first couple.

> **Point of Interest**
>
> The fact that *adam* can refer to humanity in general or to the personal name 'Adam' sets up well the relationship of Adam as the representative for the rest of humanity.

Second, covenants have conditions. The condition to this covenant relationship is set forth in the command that God gave to Adam not to eat of the tree of the knowledge of good and evil (Gen. 2:16–17). God provided everything that Adam needed for life in the garden, including water, work, and companionship in marriage. His abundant goodness was shown in allowing Adam to eat from all the trees in the garden, but he tested Adam by prohibiting him from eating from the fruit of one tree. No reason is given why Adam cannot eat from the tree of the knowledge of good and evil. This command with the penalty of death attached to it focuses on the importance of Adam obeying God in everything.

Third, covenants have blessings and curses. In Genesis 1:28 God blessed mankind and commanded them to multiply and fill the earth, to subdue it, and to have dominion over every living thing that moves on it. God's blessings are experienced in the fulfillment of God's commands. God's blessings are also seen in how God provided everything that Adam needed in the garden for a full and productive life (Gen. 2). The curse is connected to the prohibition that Adam should not eat from the tree of the knowledge of good and evil, 'for in the day you eat from it you shall surely die' (Gen. 2:17). The penalty for breaking God's command is death. If Adam and Eve disobey God's command then momentous changes would occur in their relationship with God, their relationship with each other, their relationship with creation, and their perception of themselves. Death would include physical death, but it would also have immediate spiritual implications.

Fourth, covenants operate based on a representative principle so that the actions of the covenant representative affect the others whom he represents. In every covenant, this principle includes descendants (Gen. 17:7; Deut. 5:2–3; 2 Sam. 7:12–16). The penalty clearly stated that if Adam ate from the fruit of the tree of the knowledge of good and evil, he would die. The entrance of sin and death into the world not only affected Adam and his descendants, but also creation (Gen. 2:17–18). The triumph of sin was demonstrated in the lives of the children of Adam and Eve when Cain murdered Abel. There was a separation of the ungodly line from the godly line with the intensification of sin in the boast of Lamech (Gen. 4:23–24). Not even the godly line was exempt from the result of sin as the genealogy of Adam in Genesis 5 highlights the refrain 'and he died.' Adam was the covenant head of humanity, and his sin negatively affected all of his natural descendants. Theologically, sin was imputed to (that is, sin was applied to the account of) every descendant of Adam because of Adam's transgression (Rom. 5:13). The implication is that if Adam had obeyed God's command and had passed the test, then he would have experienced further blessings. If disobedience brought death, then it is logical to conclude that obedience would mean life enjoyed with greater blessing. Adam was created in a state of positive holiness and was not subject to the law of death, but the possibility of sinning existed. He did not yet enjoy life in its fullness to the highest degree of perfection.

Fifth, covenants have signs that point to the blessings of the covenant relationship. Scholars have debated how many signs there are in Genesis 1–3 but many agree that the tree of life is a sign of the covenant. It was a pledge of the covenant of life (WLC 20), the promised reward for obedience. The fruit of this tree should not be seen as having an innate power to prolong life. Rather, it symbolized life so that when Adam forfeited the promise, he was kept from the sign (Gen. 3:22).

Point of Interest

John Murray called for a recasting of the covenant.[*] He denied there was a Covenant of Works and called the relationship between God and Adam in the garden the 'Adamic Administration.'

However, Murray did not jettison all the elements of the Covenant of Works. At the end of the day, he had a robust view of justification by faith and the imputation of Christ's righteousness to those who believe in Christ.[†]

---

[*] John Murray, *The Covenant of Grace* (P&R Publishing, 1953), p. 5.

[†] John Murray, *Redemption Accomplished and Applied* (Eerdmans, 1955), pp. 123–28

Hosea 6:7: A Covenant with Adam

Hosea 6:7 refers to God's relationship with Adam in Genesis 1–3 with the term 'covenant.' It states, 'But like Adam they transgressed the covenant; there they dealt faithlessly with me.' Some argue that 'Adam' refers to a geographical location where a transgression of the covenant took place. Evidence does not exist in Scripture that a transgression of a covenant took place at Adam. Plus, this view requires that the preposition before 'Adam' be changed from 'like' (k^e) to 'at' (b^e). The reading 'like Adam' supports the view that 'Adam' is either the general use of 'human beings' or a reference to the first human being, Adam. The general view takes away from the forceful comparison between the Israelites and Adam as covenant breakers. It is best to take 'Adam' as a reference to the first man who broke the covenant to make the point that the Israelites are covenant breakers like Adam, and they will experience similar consequences because they have broken the covenant.

QUESTIONS RELATED TO THE COVENANT OF WORKS

The Name of the Covenant

Scholars have used a variety of names for this covenant that stress different things. Some have used the term 'Covenant of Nature' because Adam's relationship with God was a natural relationship. God was the creator who created Adam as his creature. In this relationship Adam owed obedience to God, but for there to be a special relationship that offered mankind a reward for obedience, a covenant relationship was needed. WCF 7.1 states,

> The distance between God and the creature is so great, that although reasonable creatures do owe obedience unto Him as their Creator, yet they could never have any fruition of Him as their blessedness and reward, but by some voluntary condescension on God's part, which He hath been pleased to express by way of covenant.

The distinction between a natural relationship and a covenant relationship is logical and juridical, not temporal. Adam did not for a single moment exist outside of a covenant relationship with

God. Mankind could not merit anything before God based on a natural relationship alone. Thus, it seems best not to call Adam's relationship with God the Covenant of Nature.

Some have trouble with the name Covenant of Works because of possible misunderstandings associated with the term 'works.' To some, it gives the impression that the relationship between God and Adam was a commercial exchange that left Adam entirely on his own. The term Edenic Covenant has been suggested, but it can be confusing because the Covenant of Grace also begins in the Garden of Eden (Gen. 3:15). Another term for God's relationship with Adam is the Covenant of Creation. This term recognizes general aspects of the covenant that relate to the responsibilities of Adam beyond the special point of testing instituted by God. For example, God had a mission for Adam and Eve and their descendants. They had a relationship with God who was king of his creation. They experienced regular fellowship with God in the garden (Gen. 3:8). They were to expand what they had in the Garden of Eden to the ends of the earth by being fruitful, by multiplying, and by filling the earth. They would have accomplished this by exercising their kingly authority under God through ruling and subduing creation. In addition to this kingly role, they had a prophetic role to handle the Word of God correctly (Gen. 2:16) and a priestly role to guard and work the garden. These are all important aspects of Adam and Eve's role in the garden that are not opposed to the probationary test that God gave to Adam.

Point of Interest

The two verbs used in Genesis 2:15 to describe Adam's work in the garden ('to guard' [*shamar*] and 'to serve or work' [*avad*]) are also used of the Levite's work in assisting the priests in the tabernacle (Num. 3:7–8; 8:26; 18:5–6). This implies a priestly aspect to Adam's work in the garden.

The Westminster Standards affirm that the relationship between God and Adam was a covenant relationship. WCF 7.2 calls it a Covenant of Works with life offered on the condition of perfect obedience. WLC 20 and WSC 12 both state that life and death were set forth in the Covenant of Life with the tree of life offered as a pledge and the tree of the knowledge of good and evil prohibited on pain of death. The term 'Covenant of Life' emphasizes that life was the reward for Adam if he had kept the covenant. The term 'Covenant of Works' highlights that the condition of the covenant was perfect obedience. A proper understanding of works and their role in our salvation should bring to us great comfort.

The Covenant of Works and the Gospel

It is important to distinguish God's relationship with Adam before the Fall from his relationship with Adam after the Fall. Before the Fall, God condescended to Adam and entered a covenant relationship where he freely bestowed on him all kinds of gifts and favors, temporal and eternal. Some want to use the term 'grace' to describe this relationship. A better term might be benevolence (to treat someone with kindness and goodwill). Sin had not yet entered the relationship between God and Adam, so Adam did not need a mediator. Redemptive grace (to treat someone with unmerited or demerited favor) was not a factor in the relationship. When Adam sinned against God, then redemptive grace was needed for God to restore the broken relationship.

When Adam disobeyed the command that God had given to him concerning the tree of the knowledge of good and evil, the Covenant of Works formally came to an end but the obligation to perfectly fulfill the terms of the covenant remained. This obligation is implied in Genesis 3 and is clearly taught in other passages of Scripture (Gal. 3:10–14). The punishments of Genesis 3 are passed on to the descendants of Adam. The world of Cain and Abel in Genesis 4 shows the effect of sin because of Adam's transgression. Human beings are held accountable to God and are subject to death based on the terms of the original covenant. If the punishment of the broken covenant is extended to all, the covenant and the law are also extended to all. The descendants of Adam are held accountable by God for what Adam did because of the special relationship that Adam had as the representative of his descendants in the Covenant of Works. Paul makes the point in Romans 5:12–14 that even though the law had not yet been given, death reigned from Adam to Moses. Sin was in the world before the giving of the law even though sin is not counted against anyone without a law. Adam's sin was imputed to his descendants (see also 1 Cor. 15:22, 'in Adam all die'). Because no human being who is a natural descendant of Adam can keep the law perfectly, we all stand condemned (James 2:10).

Christ fulfilled the obligations of the Covenant of Works for the salvation of his people. The same obligation of personal, perfect, and perpetual obedience that God laid upon Adam, as the federal representative by the Covenant of Works, is also laid upon Christ, as the second Man and the last Adam (1 Cor. 15:45, 47). By his obedience Christ accomplished the salvation of his people who are represented by him. Thus, we can say that salvation is by works, not our works, but the works of Christ received by faith. The righteousness of Christ in keeping the law is imputed to His descendants through faith in him. Christ died on the cross as the sacrifice for sin and took upon himself the covenant curse that falls on those who break the law (Gal. 3:12–14). In this way, God can justify sinners through faith in Christ. The Covenant of Works is essential to the work of Christ as the basis for our salvation.

Warning

Some who deny the Covenant of Works see no difference between the relationship between God and Adam before the Fall and after the Fall. They hesitate to use works to characterize the relationship between God and Adam before the Fall. This can lead to a denial of the traditional view of justification by faith, including the imputation of the righteousness of Christ, and a conflation of faith and works as the basis of salvation.

Not everyone who denies that there is a Covenant of Works gets justification by faith wrong because they also affirm other key scriptural teachings, such as the contrast between the law and the gospel. The Covenant of Works is important as a foundation of the gospel, but we should rejoice when people get the gospel right even if they reject the Covenant of Works.

4

The Initiation of the Covenant of Grace

When Adam disobeyed God and broke the Covenant of Works, serious consequences followed because of the entrance of sin and death into the world. Something happened within them so that they no longer saw themselves and the world in the same way. At the end of Genesis 2 they were naked and not ashamed, but when they sinned their eyes were opened, they knew they were naked, and they were ashamed. They tried to cover their nakedness with fig leaves. Sin led to guilt, shame, and the loss of transparency. When God confronted Adam, he blamed Eve. When God confronted Eve, she blamed the serpent. Because of guilt and shame, they had trouble taking responsibility for their actions. The marriage relationship became a battlefield (Gen. 3:16). Their relationship with God was also broken. Instead of enjoying fellowship with God in the garden, they hid from God (Gen. 3:8). Sin also affected Adam and Eve's relationship to creation. The mandate to be fruitful and multiply was affected because childbearing and birth became a hard, painful process. The task of dominion over creation was affected because the ground was cursed so that working the ground for food became an arduous task (Gen. 3:17). When Adam and Eve sinned, they immediately experienced spiritual death, but physical death followed in Genesis 4–5. They also lost the special place of God's presence, the Garden of Eden, by being driven out of the garden by God (Gen. 3:23). God responds to Adam and Eve with redemptive grace by initiating the Covenant of Grace in Genesis 3.

THE UNITY OF THE COVENANT OF GRACE

The unity of the Covenant of Grace emphasizes that in the unfolding of the various Old Testament covenants there are elements that continue to be significant through redemptive history. The goal of the Covenant of Grace is that God would dwell among his people (Gen. 17:7; Exod. 6:7; 2 Sam. 7:14; Ezek. 36:28; Jer. 31:33; 2 Cor. 6:16; Rev. 21:3). There is also a unity of the people of the covenant related to the faith they share in God's promises and in a coming mediator. Although Israel is structured very differently from the church, having both a civil government and a religious administration, there is unity in the way of salvation. Such unity is expressed in the same promise of eternal life, the same mediator, and the same emphasis on faith. The apostles do not hesitate to apply terminology used in the Old Testament for Israel to the church (Gal. 3:7, 29; Phil. 3:3; 1 Pet. 2:9). In addition, there is unity in the way the covenant is administered (Rom. 11:17–24). It is also important to recognize that although the substance of the covenant is the same, there is progression in the development of the promises throughout redemptive history and in the identity of the mediator of the covenant. Each covenant will have its distinctive emphases, but the promises given in each covenant will be continued in the subsequent covenants. Finally, each covenant will also administer the blessings of that covenant to God's people so that they will experience those blessings through faith. WCF 7.5 states that the Covenant of Grace was 'for that time, sufficient and efficacious, through the operation of the Spirit, to instruct and build up the elect in faith in the promised Messiah, by whom they had full remission of sins, and eternal salvation.'

The first time that the word 'covenant' appears in Scripture is in Genesis 6:18 where God tells Noah, 'I will establish my covenant with you, and you shall come into the ark, you, your sons, your wife, and your sons' wives with you.' Normally, when a covenant is first made the verb used is 'to cut a covenant' (*karat*). In Genesis 6:18 the verb used expresses the idea 'to establish a covenant' (*qum*) which refers to the continuation of an existing covenant and not to the making of a different covenant. The previous covenant that Genesis 6:18 is referring to cannot be the Covenant of Works because the nature of the covenant with Noah is a covenant based on God's grace (Gen. 6:8), which fits the way God responded to Adam and Eve after their sin in Genesis 3. Thus, Genesis 6:18 refers to the historical initiation of the Covenant of Grace in Genesis 3. The use of 'my covenant' in Genesis 6:18 is significant because it confirms that the covenant that God began in Genesis 3 is a continuation of the covenant that God now makes with Noah. The parallels between Adam and Noah will be shown in the chapter on the covenant with Noah.

THE ELEMENTS OF THE COVENANT IN GENESIS 3

When Adam and Eve rebelled against God, fellowship with God was broken. The next time God came into the garden they hid from God (Gen. 3:8–10). Although they experienced the consequences of their sin in God's judgment, they also experienced God's redemptive grace. Their fellowship with God was broken because they had sided with the serpent in believing his lies. They needed a mediator to help restore their relationship with God. God cursed the serpent and announced the coming of a mediator in Genesis 3:15. Someone would come from the seed of the woman who would defeat the seed of the serpent. This victory would rescue a people from the power of the serpent and change their relationship with God. Instead of hostility toward God, there would be hostility between them and the serpent.* When God gave the promise of Genesis 3:15 not much was known about this coming one, but more information is given about him in the unfolding of God's revelation to follow. Early on, people were looking for the coming of this one who would give relief from painful toil because of the curse (Gen. 5:29). The New Testament clearly identifies Jesus as the seed of the woman, the son of Adam (Luke 3:38) who came to do battle with the serpent

---

Point of Interest

Not everyone confirms that Genesis 3:15 is speaking of a coming individual because the word for 'seed' (*zera*) is a collective singular, which means it could be taken as a plural referring to the descendants of the woman. John Calvin and Geerhardus Vos took this view.*

Although the term 'seed' (*zera*) is a collective singular and can refer to descendants (plural), it is clear that a single individual is in view in Genesis 3:15. When 'seed' is used with plural verbs and pronouns, then seed refers to a plurality of descendants (Gen. 17:9). When the pronouns are singular then it refers to a single individual. In Genesis 3:15 the pronouns are singular, 'he shall bruise your head and you shall bruise his heel.' Thus, this verse is referring to two individuals who will do battle with one another. The seed of the woman will be bruised on the heel, but the seed of the serpent will be bruised on the head, a fatal blow. Progressive revelation identifies the seed of the woman as Jesus Christ who will defeat the powers of Satan to secure victory for his people.

---

* John Calvin, *Genesis* (Baker, 1996), pp. 167, 170; Geerhardus Vos, *The Eschatology of the Old Testament*, ed. James T. Dennison (P&R, 2001), p. 77.

---

* Stephen G. Meyers, *Covenant Theology in Scripture: God to Us* (Grand Rapids: Reformation Heritage Books, 2021), pp. 123–24.

(Matt. 4:1–11; 8:28–34; 12:22–32), and to defeat Satan, sin, and death (Luke 10:17–20; Col. 1:13; Rev. 12:7–12).

Genesis 3:15 also shows that there will be two groups of people throughout redemptive history. The seed of the woman will trust God and believe in his promises, but the seed of the serpent will reject God and seek to live their lives apart from him. Initially, there was one community consisting of the family of Adam, but in Genesis 4 a division took place when Cain murdered his brother, Abel. As part of God's judgment, Cain was cursed and sent away from the presence of the LORD (Gen. 4:11–14). In the line of Cain, sin triumphed and then escalated in the boast of Lamech (Gen. 4:23–24). Moral autonomy ruled the day with polygamy, revenge-killing, and arrogant boasting. The other community is represented by the birth of Seth who is identified as the seed who replaced Abel. This line was the godly community who are identified as those who worship the LORD (Gen. 4:25–26). With the coming of Jesus, the division of the two communities is based on whether people believe in him. He identifies many Jews of his day as those who carry out the will of their father the devil (John 8:42–47). These two communities have different purposes and will end up in different places at the end of history (Rev. 22:14–15).

In the Covenant of Works, God offered eternal life to Adam if he would obey God. The offer of eternal life continues as a promise in the Covenant of Grace. After Adam broke the covenant, if he would have eaten from the tree of life, he would have lived forever in that sinful condition (Gen. 3:22). Part of the reason Adam was driven from the garden was to ensure that the hope of eternal life continued. The tree of life was not destroyed, but the way to it was guarded. How to partake of the tree of life will be revealed as redemptive history unfolds. Its importance is shown by its appearance in Revelation 22:2. The emphasis in Genesis 3 is on the continuation of life.

The line of the woman will continue, according to the promise of Genesis 3:15. Adam responds in faith to this promise by naming his wife Eve because she was the mother of all living (Gen. 3:20). Adam and Eve experienced the blessings of the Covenant of Grace through faith in the purposes and promises of God.

There is some debate concerning who the parties are to the Covenant of Grace. God is one of the parties but who is the second party? The Westminster Standards seem to answer this question in two ways. One answer is that the covenant is made with the elect. WSC 20 asks the question, 'Did God leave all mankind to perish in the estate of sin and misery?' The answer is,

> God having, out of his mere good pleasure, from all eternity, elected some to everlasting life, did enter into a Covenant of Grace, to deliver them out of the estate of sin and misery, and to bring them into an estate of salvation by a Redeemer.

This seems to say that the covenant was made with the elect to deliver them from their hopeless condition of sin. But then, in WLC 31, the question is asked, 'With whom was the covenant of grace made?' The answer is 'with Christ as the second Adam, and in him with all the elect as his seed.' There is no discrepancy between WSC 20 and WLC 31. The Covenant of Grace cannot be established with sinful human beings without a mediator who acts on their behalf. The work of the mediator satisfies the justice of God so that the relationship between God and sinners can be restored. The elect are in Christ and so it is appropriate that the covenant be made with Christ or with the elect.

The question of the parties to the covenant raises the issue of the character of the covenant relationship. For example, if the Covenant of Grace is made between Christ and the elect, then only the elect are in the covenant. Sections of the Westminster Standards emphasize the efficacy of the covenant for the elect who receive the benefits of the covenant (faith, the remission of sins, and eternal salvation) through the work of the Holy Spirit (WCF 7.5; WLC 32, 34; WSC 20). Here the Standards are looking at the Covenant of Grace from God's standpoint. He knows the elect and they receive the benefits of the covenant. Other sections of the Standards speak of the historical administration of the Covenant of Grace by sacraments as signs and seals of the covenant which are to be administered to believers and their children. This principle is stated in the Abrahamic Covenant (Gen. 17:7–8) and is affirmed in the New Covenant (Acts 2:39; Gal. 3:29).

The historical administration of the Covenant of Grace explains certain distinctions found in Scripture and in the Westminster Standards. There is a visible and invisible church. The visible church is defined as 'all those throughout the world that profess the true religion; and of their children and is the kingdom of our Lord Jesus Christ, the house and family of God' (WCF 25.2). There is no perfect church on earth for even 'The purest Churches under heaven are subject to both mixture and error' (WCF 25.5). The visible church includes the elect, but it also includes those who may not be the elect, whether children of believers who do not believe or those who make a false profession of faith. The Covenant of Grace has both relational and legal aspects so that a person can be part of the Covenant of Grace legally but not be in a saving relationship with God. There are legal aspects to the administration of the covenant that continue to operate in the New Covenant. Romans 11:16–24 sets forth a holiness that comes from being engrafted into the tree that is not the inward holiness that is a result of the Spirit's work in the life of a believer. This holiness is shared by all the branches that are connected to the root of the tree. The church is depicted with the same imagery as Israel because Gentiles who are engrafted in by faith can also be cut off (Rom. 11:21–22). Thus, the church should not be defined only in terms of election.

5

The Covenant with Noah

The covenant with Noah was given in relationship to the flood, which is described in Genesis 6:9–9:17. There are several challenges that must be addressed concerning this covenant. The WCF does not say much about this covenant or its role in redemptive history. There has also not been agreement on how to fit together the common grace aspects with the redemptive aspects of the covenant. Are there two covenants or just one covenant? The Covenant with Noah (also called the Noahic Covenant) is part of the outworking of the Covenant of Grace in redemptive history and is God's way of ensuring that the salvation purposes of history will not be hindered by sin.

PART OF THE COVENANT OF GRACE

When Adam and Eve rebelled against God, they experienced redemptive grace in the way God responded to their sin (see chapter 4). Life continued but sin was very prominent in the family of Adam. Cain killed his brother Abel, which led to a separation of two seeds that represented two communities. Sin escalated in the family of Cain with the arrogant boast of Lamech (Gen. 4:23–24), but the line of Seth represented the godly line associated with the worship of the LORD.

The genealogy of the godly line is given in Genesis 5 with a transition in Genesis 6:1–8 to statements about how wicked mankind had become. The wickedness of man was great, and every intention of his heart was only evil continually (v. 5). God decided to destroy humanity and the animals from the face of the earth through a flood. But, verse 8 declared, Noah had found grace (or favor) in the eyes of the LORD. In the context of wickedness that was intense, inward, pervasive, and constant, God showed grace to an individual and his family. Noah did not earn this favor but received it as a gift. After Noah received grace, he is described at the beginning of the flood narrative as a righteous man, blameless, and someone who walked with God (6:9). God's grace set Noah apart and he will carry on the godly line and save it from the judgment of the flood.

The first time the word 'covenant' (*berit*) occurs is in Genesis 6:18, in the context of God explaining to Noah how he was going to respond to the violence and corruption that had filled the earth. God is going to destroy the earth with a flood, and he wanted Noah to build an ark. Everything on earth will die, but God will establish his covenant with Noah. The normal verb for making a covenant is 'to cut a covenant' (*karat*). The use of the verb 'establish' (*qum*) shows that Genesis 6:18 is referring to a covenant God had already made with Adam. Because God responded to Noah with grace (Gen. 6:8), the previous covenant that is being referenced must be God's response to Adam after the Fall. Although Adam and Eve rebelled against God, he responded to their sin with grace (see chapter 4). But not only does Genesis 6:18 look back to a previous covenant that was characterized by redemptive grace, it also looks forward to the covenant God will establish with Noah. The Noahic Covenant is an outworking of the Covenant of Grace.

ONE COVENANT OR TWO?

The distinctive characteristic of the covenant with Noah is that the covenant was established not only with Noah, his family, and their descendants (Gen. 6:18, 9:9) but also with the animals on the ark (Gen. 9:10) and with the earth (Gen. 9:13). Another way to say this is that there are both redemptive grace and common grace elements in the covenant with Noah. The redemptive aspects include: the evidence in Noah's life of divine grace (Gen. 6:8–9, 22); the fact that God works through the family of Noah as the godly line; the worship of God through the offering of sacrifices (Gen. 8:20–21); and the separation of the godly from the ungodly line after the flood (Gen. 9:24–27). There are also common grace elements in the covenant with Noah that are broader than the covenant community. They include: the preservation of the created order (Gen. 8:22); the institution of family (Gen. 9:1) and state (Gen. 9:5–6); and the continuation of dominion (Gen. 9:2–3). The sign of the covenant was the rainbow, which is a reminder that God will never destroy the earth again with a flood (Gen. 9:16). Part of the purpose of the Noahic Covenant was the continuation of life on earth so that God's redemptive purposes can be accomplished. This covenant preserves humanity and the earth until the final judgment.

> **Point of Interest**
>
> Meredith Kline sees two covenants in the account of the flood. He sees a redemptive covenant in Genesis 6:13–8:22 which he connects with Genesis 3:15. He also sees a common grace covenant in Genesis 9:1–17 which he connects with Genesis 3:16–19.[*]
>
> ---
>
> [*] For a defense of Kline's view see Miles Van Pelt, 'The Noahic Covenant of the Covenant of Grace,' in *Covenant Theology*, eds. Guy P. Waters, et al., pp. 111–32.

Although the covenant with Noah contains both redemptive and common grace elements, there are not two covenants (a redemptive covenant and a common grace covenant) but one covenant that expresses both elements. Several reasons support this view. The redemptive elements and the common grace elements cannot be neatly separated from each other but are woven together throughout the account of the flood (Gen. 6:9–9:17). For example, when God first told Noah that he would establish his covenant with Noah and his family, he also mentioned that Noah would bring into the ark different kinds of animals, two of every sort, to keep them alive (Gen. 6:19–20). In the section that emphasizes common grace elements, God mentions that he is establishing his covenant with Noah and his offspring and with every living creature (Gen. 9:9–10) and continues to repeat that he has made this covenant with you and every living creature (Gen. 9:10, 12, 15). The pronoun 'you' in these verses is plural, which means it includes Noah and his family and their descendants.* The fact that Noah and his family would be mentioned in Genesis 9 argues for one covenant with two elements of redemptive and common grace.

The use of 'my covenant' throughout the flood account also emphasizes that there is one covenant. The phrase 'my covenant' first occurs in Genesis 6:18 and refers to the covenant that God made with Adam after the sin of Adam and Eve. But it also looks forward to the covenant God will establish with Noah. The phrase 'my covenant' also occurs in Genesis 9:9, 11, and 15, which shows that this is the same covenant as mentioned in Genesis 6:18. Furthermore, the use of the rainbow in later passages of Scripture appears in passages that emphasize God's covenant faithfulness to his people (Ezek. 1:28). The rainbow

---

* The singular use of 'you' in Gen. 6:18–21 focuses on Noah as the one who is the focal point to continue the covenant of grace started in Genesis 3 (Myers, *God to Us*, p. 131).

shows up again in Revelation 4:3 and 10:1 in reference to the consummation of the covenantal purposes of God to preserve his people in the middle of judgment as they stand in the presence of their covenant God.[*]

THE JUDGMENT OF THE FLOOD

The flood destroys all animals and humans living on the earth who had the breath of life (Gen. 7:21–22). The ungodly line perished but God saved Noah and his family in the ark. The flood brought the earth into a state of chaos that resembled the state of the earth as uninhabitable (formless and void) at the beginning of Genesis 1. In fact, there are clear parallels to the creation account throughout this section of Genesis. Instead of the declaration that God saw that everything was good, as in Genesis 1, God saw that the wickedness of mankind was great on the earth and that their hearts were only evil continually (Gen. 6:5). In Genesis 1, the Spirit of God was hovering over the face of the waters before the earth became a place where mankind could live. In Genesis 6:3, God's Spirit is mentioned but in a context of judgment that was going to fall upon the earth ending the life of mankind. In Genesis 1, there was a movement from chaos (the formless and void state of the earth) to order, by the separation and gathering of the waters (Gen. 1:6–10). In the flood, the disorder of judgment is brought about by the unleashing of waters that cover the earth (Gen. 7:17–23). The flood brings the earth into a state of not being habitable for humanity or any other life that existed on the earth (Gen. 7:21–23). Although all life outside the ark perished, God saved Noah and his family from destruction. God protected Noah by shutting him in the ark (7:16) and God remembered Noah by causing the flood waters to recede (8:1).

---

[*] Meyers, *God to Us*, pp. 140–41.

God then brought the earth into a state where it was habitable again for human beings. A wind (ruach) blew over the earth and the waters of the flood subsided (Gen. 8:1), just like the Spirit (ruach) was hovering over the waters in Genesis 1:2. There is a renewed separation of the land and sea (Gen. 1:7 and 8:3, 7, 13) with the appearance of dry land again (Gen. 1:9 and 8:14).

GOD'S COVENANT WITH NOAH

Although there are redemptive elements in 8:20–9:17, there is an emphasis on the continuation of the common grace elements in the operation of creation. When Noah left the ark, he built an altar to the LORD and offered burnt offerings on the altar. This act of worship was pleasing to God, and he promised never again to destroy every living creature on the earth with a flood. The rationale for never cursing the ground this way again is stated in verse 21, 'for the intention of man's heart is evil from his youth.' This seems like a strange rationale, but it recognizes that the sinfulness of humanity will continue and that the sin problem will never be cured by judgment and curse. The earth must be preserved so that God's plan of salvation can be fulfilled.

God promised to continue the order of creation so that seedtime and harvest, cold and night, summer and winter, day and night would not cease (Gen. 1:14 and 8:22). God also promised to continue the mandate that God had given Adam and Eve to be fruitful, multiply, and fill the earth. Noah is presented as a second Adam as he and his family are given the same commands that Adam and Eve were given but with the recognition of the existence of sin. They were to be fruitful and multiply on the earth (Gen. 8:17), which is repeated in Genesis 9:1 with the addition that they were to fill the earth (Gen. 1:28). This assumed that the institution of marriage given in Genesis 2:24 is still relevant. Human dominion over creation is also affirmed but with the recognition that animals will fear human beings as God gave animals to human beings for food (Gen. 9:3). In Genesis 1:26–28 human beings were made in God's image and the implication of the sanctity of life is affirmed in Genesis 9:6. This laid the foundation of government and established capital punishment as an appropriate response to murder. God started over with the family of Noah to see if this second opportunity to carry out his purposes for creation would be any more successful.

God confirmed his commitment to creation and to Noah, as the representative of mankind, by means of a covenant. The sign of this covenant was a rainbow. It primarily stood as a reminder to God of his covenant commitments (Gen. 9:15–16). Twice God states, 'I will remember' when he sees the rainbow in the clouds. For God to remember the covenant means that he will act to fulfill his covenant promise to never destroy the world again with a flood. The rainbow is a universal sign that all can see because the covenant with Noah is a covenant made with all creation. The term for 'rainbow' (*qeshet*) also refers to the bow used as a weapon. Instead of a symbol of combat it is a symbol of peace.

The universal aspect of the Noahic Covenant means that the elements that are integral to the unity of the covenant of grace are highlighted in different ways. The covenant with Noah promised the continuation of life so that the promise of eternal life could be fulfilled. The flood did not solve the problem of sin (Gen. 9:18–29) but the godly line was preserved so that the mediator promised in Genesis 3:15 could come. One of the main purposes of the Noahic Covenant was to provide for the continuation of creation so God's redemptive purpose of salvation under the Covenant of Grace could be carried out.

THE FLOOD IN THE NEW TESTAMENT

The events associated with Noah's flood are used to explain both judgment and redemptive aspects of salvation. The global judgment of the undoing of creation makes the flood a fitting picture of the end of the world. The people of Noah's day carried on their normal lives of eating, drinking, and marriage without any awareness of the coming flood of judgment until suddenly the flood came and their lives were swept away (Matt. 24:38; Luke 17:27). The people who are alive when the Son of Man comes will experience the same thing. They will not be aware of the coming of Christ until suddenly, he comes, and it will be too late. Such a pattern is typical of unbelievers who live their lives without understanding the danger they are in apart from Christ. Jesus uses the flood to warn people of his coming.

Peter uses Noah and the flood to support his teaching of the perseverance and suffering of Christians. Peter warns against the danger of false teachers in 2 Peter and encourages Christians with the reality that God will destroy such teachers. He uses Noah and the flood twice to show that their coming destruction is certain (2 Pet. 2:5; 3:6). Just like in the flood, none of the wicked will be able to escape the judgment, except this time it will be by fire.

Peter had already used the deliverance of Noah in the flood to speak of salvation (1 Pet. 3:18–22). He encouraged the Christians who were suffering because of their good behavior in Christ by reminding them that Christ also suffered unjustly for their salvation and that God brought Noah and his family safely through the flood waters. The reference to salvation through water brought to Peter's mind baptism, which corresponds to the flood, and 'now saves you.' There is a typological relationship between the waters of the flood and the waters of baptism. The focus of Peter is on salvation because he specifically mentions the cleansing nature of baptism. It is not the ritual of baptism that saves because water can only remove dirt from the body, but it is the inner renewal that comes from Christ. The work of Christ is the basis for the renewal of the believer with the water of baptism pointing to that reality.

6

The Covenant with Abraham

After the flood the problem of sin continued not only in the family of Noah, the godly line (Gen. 9:20–27), but also in the ungodly line in the Tower of Babel (Gen. 11:1–9). This incident was a clear case of rebellion against God and a refusal to fill the earth by staying in one place to make a name for themselves. The call of Abram was God's response to the growth of sin and was a demonstration of God's grace. Although the godly line went through Shem and Peleg to Terah, the father of Abram (Gen. 11:10–26), the effect of sin is seen in the later statement by Joshua that Terah served other gods (Josh. 24:2). God graciously called Abram out of a pagan background to follow him.

THE PROMISES OF GOD

God's relationship with Abram is developed in several stages. First, God called Abram to leave his country, his family, and the security of his father's house to go to a land he had not seen (Gen. 12:1–3). God also made several promises to Abram if he would follow God's call. He promised to make him into a great nation. For this promise to be fulfilled at least one child would need to be born to Abram and Sarai. The two promises of land and seed dominate the story. God also promised to make the name of Abram great in direct contrast to the Tower of Babel incident where people tried to make a great name for themselves. God also promised to bless Abram. The word 'blessing' occurs five times in Genesis 12:1–3. This matches the five times the word 'curse' occurred in Genesis 1–11 (Gen. 3:14, 17; 4:11; 5:29; 9:25). God will bless Abram and his descendants to counter the curse of sin prominent in the first eleven chapters of Genesis. God not only promises to bless Abram, but also to bless those who are a blessing to him and to curse anyone who seeks to dishonor or harm him. Ultimately, the blessing of God will come to all the families of the earth through Abram and his descendants. God moves from the universal setting of Genesis 1–11 to focus on one man and his family with the purpose to bring blessing to the whole world.

THE COVENANT CEREMONY

God made promises to Abram in Genesis 12 concerning land and seed. Genesis 12–14 focuses on the promises of land and Genesis 16–22 focuses on the promise of seed. Both promises come together in Genesis 15 where the covenant God made with Abram is described. God appeared to Abram in a vision and reminded him that he was the one who gave him protection and security and that his reward would be great (15:1). Abram responded by reminding God that the promise of an offspring had not yet been fulfilled and suggested that his servant Eliezer should become his heir. God rejected Abram's proposal and emphasized that Abram's own son will be his heir. He showed him the innumerable stars of heaven and proclaimed, 'So shall your offspring be' (15:5). Abram believed God's promise and 'he counted it to him as righteousness' (15:6). This is not the first time that Abram has trusted God's Word (12:1–3), but his faith is mentioned here because of the significance of the promise of innumerable descendants considering Abram's continuing childlessness.

God also raised the issue of land by stating, 'I am the LORD who brought you out from the Ur of the Chaldeans to give you this land to possess' (15:7). Abram responded with a question concerning how he would know that he would possess the land. God secured the promises he made to Abram with a covenant ceremony (15:9–21). Abram was told to bring several animals, to cut them in half, and to lay the halves over against each other (15:9–10). As the sun went down, he fell into a deep sleep and 'a dreadful and great darkness fell upon him' (15:12). God informed Abram that his descendants would be afflicted for four hundred years, but then he would bring them out of that land to give them the land of Canaan. It would occur when the iniquity of the inhabitants of Canaan was complete. The covenant ceremony included a statement of the promises (15:13–16) and a description of the boundaries of the land and its inhabitants (15:18–21). The promise of land will be fulfilled even though it will be fulfilled in the future.

Normally in this covenant ceremony, both parties of the covenant would pass through the slain animals cut in two. The purpose of this would be to acknowledge that if either party did not keep the terms of the covenant, they were putting themselves under the curse of the covenant, represented by the animals cut in half. What is remarkable about the ceremony in Genesis 15 is that only God walks through the slain animals. The smoking pot and the flaming torch symbolize the presence of God as they pass between the animals. God allowed himself to be bound by covenant obligation to show that he was serious about keeping the covenant promises.

THE CONFIRMATION OF THE COVENANT

In Genesis 15 God committed himself to fulfill his covenant promises to Abram but it was also important how Abram and his descendants responded to God and his promises. Abram was in a relationship with God and had already demonstrated trust in God by his obedience. Although not perfect (Gen. 12:10–20), he had consistently lived a life of faith since the call of God, and he responded with faith in response to God's assurance that he would fulfill his promises (Gen. 15:6). The importance of how Abram and his descendants responded to God is demonstrated in Genesis 16–17.

In Genesis 16, Abram and Sarai did not trust the promise of God that an heir would be born to them. The theme of an offspring (seed) dominates Genesis 16–22, even framing this section (16:1; 22:17). The statement at the beginning of chapter 16, that Sarai had not borne any children, stands in sharp contrast to the promise of chapter 15, that their descendants would be innumerable as the stars of heaven. Sarai became impatient and came up with a plan of her own to produce an heir. She offered her Egyptian servant to Abram so that 'it may be that I shall obtain children by her' (16:2). Although such a practice was common to the culture of that day, it stood sharply opposed to God's promise that a son born to Abram and Sarai would be their heir (15:4). This plan went against the promise of God. They devised a human plan based on their own efforts to try to solve the problem of Sarai's barrenness. Sarai was getting older and was even past the normal age of bearing children, but instead of trying to solve this problem through human effort they should have trusted in the power of God to fulfill his covenant promise that they would have a son. By trusting in their own plan, dissension came into the household. Sarai lost respect, Hagar lost a home, and Abram was caught in the middle of a quarrel between two women (16:4–6).

In Genesis 17, the importance of responding in faith to God's promises is highlighted when God confirmed the promise of an heir through a covenant sign that Abram and his descendants must keep. Genesis 16 ends with the age of Abram as eighty-six years old. Genesis 17 begins by stating that Abram was ninety-nine years old. There are thirteen years of silence between the birth of Ishmael to Hagar and God's appearance to Abram. Failure to bring about the promised heir through human, natural means does not destroy the covenant promise. God identified himself as 'God Almighty' (17:1), which showed he had the power to fulfill the promise of an heir through Abram and Sarai. He then exhorted Abram with two imperatives, 'walk before me and be blameless' (17:1), which emphasized Abram's faithfulness and obedience.

Genesis 17 should be understood as a confirmation of the covenant promises that God had already made to Abram and not as a second covenant. The promises of blessing, seed, and land in Genesis 17:5–8 are the same promises God made in Genesis 12 and 15. The need for a covenant sign to confirm God's promises was demonstrated by the lack of faith in Genesis 16. The terminology in Genesis 17 supports the view it is a confirmation of promises already given. The characteristic phrase for entering a covenant relationship ('to cut a covenant') is not used in chapter 17 as it is in 15:18. The phrase 'that I may make my covenant between me and you' uses the verb 'to give, set' (*natan*), which is the verb used in Genesis 9:12–13 for the appointment of the rainbow as a sign of the covenant with Noah. The statement 'my covenant is with you' (Gen. 17:4) refers to an ongoing covenant relationship. The phrase 'I will establish my covenant' (*qum*) confirms there is already a covenant relationship (17:7). God had called him, and he had responded in faith. Considering his disobedience to God in Genesis 16, God called him to obedience in Genesis 17. Having been declared righteous by God through faith in Genesis 15 (justification), he must continue to live in a way that is pleasing to God in Genesis 17 (sanctification).

Further confirmation of the fulfillment of the promises of God is that both Abram and Sarai are given new names that set forth what God promised to accomplish. The name 'Abram' means 'exalted father' and the new name 'Abraham' means 'father of a multitude.' Every time Abraham hears his new name he will be reminded of this promise of God. Sarai's name is changed to Sarah. Both of these names mean 'princess.' Perhaps her birth name looks back on her noble descent and her new name looks forward to her noble descendants.* This fits God's promise that her descendants will become nations, with kings of peoples coming from her (Gen. 17:16). Further confirmation comes in Genesis 17:7 where God promises he will be a God to Abraham and his descendants, who will one day inherit the land of Canaan.

> **Point of Interest**
>
> The promise to 'you and your offspring' (Gen. 17:7) is a promise that continues into the New Covenant. Every covenant includes descendants. Peter makes this connection on the day of Pentecost when he proclaimed to a Jewish audience that the promise is to you and your children. Paul also addressed children as part of the covenant community in Ephesians 6:1-3.

Abraham responded in faith to the covenant promise by circumcising Ishmael and all the men of his household, including himself. Circumcision was the sign of the covenant but to what did it point? As common with covenants, there were both blessings and curses associated with the covenant. The blessings of the covenant included the promises that

---

* Bruce K. Waltke, *Genesis: A Commentary* (Grand Rapids: Zondervan Academic, 2001), p. 262.

God had made to Abram in Genesis 12 and reflected the spiritual relationship that Abraham already had with God (Gen. 15:6 and 17:2). Later passages in Scripture will emphasize circumcision of the heart (Deut. 10:16; 30:6), a fitting phrase to show that circumcision was not just a physical act but pointed to a spiritual relationship. Paul confirms this in Romans 4:11, 'He received the sign of circumcision as a seal of the righteousness that he had by faith while he was still uncircumcised.' Circumcision was both a sign and seal of the righteousness Abraham received by faith. Circumcision was a sign of the covenant (Gen. 17:11) pointing to the relationship established with Abraham by God through faith (Gen. 15:6). Circumcision was also a seal of the covenant which guaranteed that righteousness will be given to Abraham's descendants based on faith. Abraham experienced the benefit of this sign

---

Point of Interest

The Colossians were circumcised with a circumcision made without hands, which corresponds to the circumcision of the heart in the Old Testament (Col. 2:11–12). Circumcision was a sign and seal of the Abrahamic Covenant pointing to the spiritual reality of a cleansed heart (Deut. 30:6) and guaranteeing that the response of faith would lead to salvation (Gen. 15:6; Rom. 4:11). Baptism functions the same way for the New Covenant and so should be administered to the children of believers.

Circumcision did not just function as a genealogical principle to mark an ethnic people but operated according to a federal principle administered to all those under the authority of Abraham, including his servants (Gen. 17:23). In the New Testament household baptisms, the issue is not whether infants were present or others in the household believed, but that all who were under the authority of the one who believed were baptized.*

---

* Myers, *God To Us*, p. 301.

through faith and all his descendants will also experience this spiritual blessing through faith. The covenant of circumcision administered the gospel promise of the evangelical reality of justification by faith. There were also earthly and temporal blessings promised in the covenant. These blessings had a higher purpose because they were types of the benefits that God would one day grant to his people in the consummation.

The promise of a seed in Genesis 3:15 is advanced in the Abrahamic Covenant. Isaac is the promised seed and through his descendants the promises of the covenant will continue. There is an emphasis in Genesis 17 on one seed (one heir) with many descendants. The covenant will be established with Isaac (17:9), but it will also include the descendants of Abraham as the ones who will receive the promise of land (17:8). It is also significant that the word for 'seed' is a collective singular that can refer to one offspring or many descendants. These principles become important for later discussions of the covenant for the New Covenant will also include descendants (Acts 2:39). Paul connects the promise to Abraham that 'In you shall all the nations be blessed' as being fulfilled in the New Covenant in the preaching of the gospel to the Gentiles (Gal. 3:8).

7

The Covenant with Moses

The Covenant with Moses is the most difficult covenant to understand because it has many aspects. Minor differences of emphases can affect one's understanding and explanation of this covenant. Prominent Reformed scholars have disagreed on its nature and character. This chapter will seek to explain the meaning of the Covenant with Moses (also called the Mosaic Covenant), its relationship to the Covenant of Grace, and its role in redemptive history.

THE HISTORICAL CONTEXT OF THE COVENANT WITH MOSES

God had made certain promises to Adam and Abraham as part of the Covenant of Grace and by the end of Genesis and the beginning of Exodus God was at work to fulfill those promises. The promise of a seed who would come (Gen. 3:15) narrows down from the line of Abraham to the family of Judah with an emphasis on a victorious king (Gen. 49:8–12). The promise of innumerable descendants (Gen. 15:5; 17:6) begins to be fulfilled in the land of Egypt where even in the middle of oppression, language from the creation account is used to describe Israel in Egypt, 'But the people of Israel were *fruitful*, increased greatly;

they *multiplied* and grew exceedingly strong, so that the land was *filled* with them' (Exod. 1:7; emphasis added to show the relationship with Gen. 1:28).

God had promised to make Abraham's name great (Gen. 12:2) and the rise of Joseph to power as the second in command in Egypt is a partial fulfillment of this promise. He was also a blessing to the nations by providing food during the seven years of famine. God's promise to curse those who mistreat Abraham's descendants (Gen. 12:3) will be demonstrated by God delivering Israel from Egypt through the plagues. The promise of land (Gen. 12:1) is still in the future, but God will deliver his people to bring them to the land he had promised them (Gen. 50:24). The promises of the Abrahamic covenant are the reason for God's action when his people cry to him for help from their bondage in Egypt (Exod. 2:23–25). God heard their groaning and remembered his covenant with Abraham, Isaac, and Jacob. He had not forgotten his covenant promises but the time had come for him to act on those promises by sending Moses as the one who would deliver them from Egypt.

THE RATIFICATION OF THE COVENANT WITH MOSES

In Exodus 19 the Israelites arrived at Mt. Sinai where they would enter a covenant with God to become a nation, to receive his law (Exod. 19–24) and a system of worship that would lead to the presence of God dwelling with them (Exod. 25–40). Exodus 19 prepared the people to receive the law of God and to enter the covenant. God appeared to Moses in a thick cloud so that the people would listen to God through Moses (19:9). The people were to be set apart and cleansed in preparation for God's appearing. Because of God's presence on the mountain the people were prohibited from touching it lest they die (19:12–13). On the third day, they stood at the foot of the mountain where God appeared in smoke and fire so that the whole mountain trembled (19:18). The seriousness of entering into a relationship with God is emphasized. The people needed a mediator to intercede for them and to speak to them the Word of God (19:9). The people must be willing to obey God's voice and to keep the covenant he will make with them (19:5), an obedience that flows from a heart that properly fears God (20:20).

If the people respond appropriately to God, they would not only experience the benefit of a covenant relationship with God, but they would also fulfill his promises for them (Exod. 19:5–6). Three terms are used to describe Israel's unique relationship with God. They will be a treasured possession (*segullah*). This word refers to a king's personal treasure and shows that Israel will be the LORD's unique, prized possession. The other two terms describe the mediatorial role Israel will have toward the nations. As a kingdom of priests, Israel will worship God and seek to extend the worship and presence of God to the nations. As a holy nation, Israel will demonstrate the blessings that come in being in a relationship with God. He promises to pour out abundant blessings on his people (Deut. 7:8–16; 28:1–14) so that she can influence the nations and draw them to the God she worships.

Already in Exodus 19:8 the people committed themselves to do all that the LORD had spoken to them. God moved forward with his covenant purposes by giving Israel his law (Exod. 20:1–23:19), reminding them of the promise to conquer the land of Canaan (Exod. 23:20–33), and ratifying the covenant through a covenant ceremony (Exod. 24:1–18). The main elements of the ceremony included the building of an altar, erecting twelve stone pillars, offering animal sacrifices, applying blood to the people, and the reading of the covenant (24:4–8). The altar was needed for the animal sacrifices. Throwing half the blood on the altar committed the LORD to keep his part of the covenant. The twelve stone pillars served as witnesses to remind the people of their commitment. Animal sacrifices were common in covenant ceremonies emphasizing death if the covenant is broken. The terms of the covenant were put into writing as part of its ratification. When Moses read the Book of the Covenant to the people, they verbally committed themselves to keep it through obedience to the law. At that point, Moses sprinkled the blood from the animal sacrifices on the people declaring, 'Behold, the blood of the covenant that the LORD has made with you in accordance with these words' (24:8). The people were bound by oath to honor God by keeping the covenant, which would lead to life, but breaking the covenant would lead to death. The covenant ceremony ended in a meal with seventy elders of Israel to confirm agreement to the covenant (24:9–11). God's presence was also manifested to them in that he allowed them to behold him to show that he was a willing partner to the covenant and desired to be in this relationship.

THE DISTINCTIVE ELEMENT OF THE COVENANT WITH MOSES

At Mt. Sinai, Israel became a nation to fulfill the mission God had given to her (Exod. 23:20–33). It is not surprising that God would give the law to govern the covenant relationship and to help Israel know how to live in a way that is pleasing to God. The law is the distinctive element of the Mosaic Covenant, and it is important to understand how the law functions. Two different types of law are given to Israel: the Ten Commandments and the covenant code (laws which apply the Ten Commandments to the life of the people). The Ten Commandments are absolute statements of what should or should not be done (Exod. 20:1–17). They have no social context or penalties associated with them and are closely identified with the covenant itself (Deut. 4:13). They were written by the finger of God on two tablets of stone (Exod. 31:18). They come from God to Israel directly which sets them apart from the other laws in the Mosaic Covenant and gives them priority. The other laws are case laws that apply the Ten Commandments to various situations (Exod. 20:22–23:19). They give insight into Israel's social relationships and are accompanied with penalties that accompany the breaking of them. The case law is mediated through Moses to the people. The Ten Commandments are primary, and the case law is derivative with a focus on the application of the law to Israel.

God gave the law to Israel in the context of redemption, 'I am the Lord your God, who brought you out of the land of Egypt, out of the house of slavery' (Exod. 20:2). Having been redeemed by God, the

> **Point of Interest**
>
> There were two tablets of stone not because the Ten Commandments could not fit on one tablet. Whenever a covenant was made one copy of the covenant was kept in the suzerain's (conquering king) sanctuary and one copy was placed in the vassal's (conquered king and people) sanctuary as a testimony to them. In the covenant that God made with Israel, both copies were kept in the ark of the covenant.

law functioned to show Israel how to live in a way that would demonstrate their faith and trust in God (the third use of the law). Israel's obedience is related to the mission that God had given to her. Moses reminds the people in Deuteronomy that the law was given and they should obey it in the land that God was giving them. Keeping the law would demonstrate their wisdom and understanding in the sight of all the peoples who would recognize that God had made them into a great nation through the beneficial righteousness of the law he had given them (4:6–8). Israel's obedience would show to the surrounding nations the character of the God they worshipped and would draw the nations to worship God. As God's people trust in God the law functions as a great blessing to them to help them grow in their relationship with him (sanctification) and they are enabled to fulfill their mission to the nations.

Whenever God's people reject him or turn away from him in unbelief, they are in danger of experiencing the judgment of covenant curse because of their disobedience. This use of the law, called the second use, shows us how far short we fall from God's standard of righteousness and that we need a mediator and a sacrifice to atone for our sins. Covenant judgment should have led Israel to repent of her disobedience and to turn back to God for his provision of forgiveness. The problem was that Israel as a nation and most of her kings continued to live in ways that were displeasing to God, which led to God's judgment.

> **Point of Interest**
> There are different ways that the uses of the law are numbered. In the Formula of Concord 6 (Lutheran), the first use refers to the role of the law to restrain evil in society; the second use, to showing us our failures and the need of a redeemer; and the third use, as a guide for showing God's people how to live in a way that is pleasing to God. This numbering is followed in this book. Calvin has the same three uses but reverses the first two (*Institutes of the Christian Religion* 2/7/6–13).

The prophets warned God's people and kings of the coming judgment based on the curses of the covenant (Lev. 26:14–45; Deut. 28:15–68), which led to the destruction and exile of the northern kingdom in 722 B.C. by the Assyrians and the southern kingdom in 587 B.C. by the Babylonians.

Both second and third uses are part of the function of the law. Sometimes the emphasis is on obedience (Exod. 19:5) and sometimes the emphasis is on God's elective love

(Deut. 7:6–8). Sometimes God's law is presented as the life of the people (Deut. 4:5–8) and sometimes as the instrument of judgment (Deut. 29:24–28). Whether a law is second or third use depends on the condition of a person before God. In fact, any moral law can be either second or third use. Paul uses the seventh commandment as both second use (Rom. 7:7) and third use (Rom. 13:8–10). If an Israelite is not a believer or is not concerned about living in a way that pleases God by keeping the law, then the second use of the law is important. If an Israelite is a believer and is seeking to live their life in trust and obedience to God, the third use is important. These principles also apply to Israel as a nation and to the king as her representative.

The second use of the law presupposes that the requirement of the Covenant of Works to keep the law perfectly is still an obligation that must be met by people. The penalty for breaking the law shows that the requirement of the law is perfect obedience for someone to inherit eternal life. Of course, no one can keep the law perfectly, so everyone stands condemned under the just requirements of the law. A mediator is needed who can keep the law perfectly to pay the penalty for when the law is broken. The revelation of the law is intended to lead to the necessity of atonement. Paul himself understood the law in this way (Rom. 10:5; Gal. 3:12). In Romans 10:5 he argues that there is a righteousness based on the law that is contrasted with a righteousness based on faith. Paul references Leviticus 18:5 in Romans 10:5, as he does in Galatians 3:12, for the principle that there is a righteousness based on the law. There are two ways to earn righteousness before God, the way of law/works and the way of faith, and both are proved from Old Testament texts.

The Westminster Standards agree with this use of the law as demonstrated in the proof texts. WCF 7.2 states that 'life was promised to Adam ... upon the condition of personal and perfect obedience' and the reference for this statement is Galatians 3:12 and Romans 10:5 because both use Leviticus 18:5 to establish the principle 'do this and live.' WCF 19.2 states that, 'This law, after his fall, continued to be a perfect rule of righteousness; and, as such, was delivered by God upon Mt. Sinai.' The emphasis here on the second use of the law does not negate the third use of the law. The former refers to justification and the latter to sanctification.

THE COVENANT WITH MOSES AS PART OF THE COVENANT OF GRACE

The Mosaic Covenant is part of the outworking of the Covenant of Grace and was necessary for the promises of the Abrahamic Covenant to be fulfilled. Israel had to be organized as a nation to take the land that God had promised to Abraham's descendants. Once the land was taken, the other promises could be fulfilled. During the kingdom of Solomon, Israel's name became great because the descendants of Abraham became as many as the sand of the sea (Gen. 22:17; 1 Kings 4:20). They also became a blessing to the nations as kings and rulers came to see the wonders of the kingdom of Solomon (1 Kings 4:21; 10:1–13). Of course, this was not the final fulfillment of God's promises to Abraham because Solomon's heart was turned away from the Lord and the division of the kingdom followed. The Mosaic Covenant did not supplant or annul the Abrahamic Covenant because the promises of the Abrahamic Covenant remained in force. The use of 'my covenant' in Genesis 6:18 (Noah), 17:2 (Abraham), and Exodus 19:5 (Moses) shows the unity of the Covenant of Grace and that the Mosaic Covenant should be seen as a further outworking of the Covenant of Grace.

As part of the Covenant of Grace, the Mosaic Covenant is concerned with Israel's spiritual relationship with God. The sacrifices and rituals of cleansing (the types and shadows) of the Mosaic Covenant are geared toward furthering the people's spiritual life and enabling God to continue to dwell in their midst. And yet, the results of keeping or breaking the Mosaic Covenant primarily focus on temporal and material blessings and curses (Lev. 26; Deut. 28). These are part of the types and symbols of the Mosaic Covenant that point to other realities both spiritual and material. The land of Canaan is a type of the new heavens and new earth so that the physical blessings of the Mosaic Covenant will be experienced by God's people in a form that is appropriate to their glorified existence. The physical curse of judgment will fall on unbelievers who will experience the curse in both spiritual and physical ways appropriate to their eternal existence. But the blessings and curses of the Mosaic Covenant are not limited to the new heavens and new earth because they have relevance for God's people today. WCF 19:6 recognizes that true believers are not under the law as a Covenant of Works, but the law can still be of great use to them to inform them of the will of God and their duty to God (third use) and to show them the pollutions of their heart and their need of Christ (second use). It goes on to mention the threatenings of the law (the curses) and the promises of

---

Point of Interest

Some Reformed covenant theologians understand the Mosaic Covenant as a republication of the Covenant of Works because it is viewed as operating according to a similar probationary-works principle (in a typological sense). In this view, Israel's situation parallels Adam's situation in the Covenant of Works because whether Israel keeps the inheritance of land depends on works according to the law and not faith according to the promise.[*]

---

[*] Meredith Kline, *God, Heaven, and Har Magedon* (Wipf & Stock, 2006), p. 127. For more on Kline's view see Belcher, *The Fulfillment of the Promises of God*, pp. 176–79, 186–90.

blessings. For the regenerate, the threatenings show what their sins deserve and what afflictions in this life they may expect even though they are free from the curse threatened in the law by the work of Christ. Even though believers have no fear of eternal punishment for sin, there can be temporal judgments related to the consequences of sin (1 Cor. 11:32; WCF 17.3). WCF 19.6 also states that the promises of the covenant show believers God's approval of obedience and what blessings they may expect when they obey even though those blessings are not due to them by law as a Covenant of Works. The Old Testament emphasizes material blessings without ignoring spiritual blessings. The New Testament emphasizes spiritual blessings without ignoring physical blessings The new heavens and earth will have an abundance of both. Thus, believers in the New Covenant can benefit from the teaching of the blessings and curses of the Mosaic Covenant.

8

The Covenant with David

God's covenant with David represents the culmination of all the promises of the previous covenants. It not only consolidates those promises but also sets the stage for the further outworking of them in Old Testament history and for their fulfillment in Christ. The Covenant with David (also called the Davidic Covenant) is a high point in Old Testament theology because it advances prior Old Testament concepts to a new stage apart from which the hope of a coming king cannot be understood. God's purposes to redeem a people reach a climactic stage in the Old Testament. The kingdom of God arrives in a formal manner with indications of how God will rule among His people. God situates his throne in a single locality and the Davidic line is established as the line through which God will exercise his rule on the earth.

GOD'S PROMISES TO DAVID (2 SAMUEL 7)

In 2 Samuel 7 David was secure in his kingdom, living in his house, and he enjoyed rest from his enemies (2 Sam. 7:1–3). David had been made king over all Israel and had moved his capital to Jerusalem (2 Sam. 5). David had also brought the ark of God, the visible symbol of God's presence, to Jerusalem (2 Sam. 6). With the ark of God in Jerusalem and with David experiencing rest from his enemies, it seemed appropriate to honor God by building him a house of cedar wherein the ark of God would dwell. At first the prophet Nathan gave his blessing to this idea, but then the LORD told Nathan there were reasons that David was not the one to build the temple (2 Sam. 7:4–17). This work would be carried out by his son. God had something greater planned for David. Instead of David building a house/temple (*bayit*) for God, God will build a house/dynasty (*bayit*) for David. This promise is the focus of 2 Samuel 7 around which the basic elements of God's other promises to David are given. Although 2 Samuel 7 does not use the term covenant to describe this relationship, other passages identify it as a covenant (2 Sam. 23:5; Ps. 89:3, 28, 34; 132:12). God gave to David an enduring, unconditional promise, sworn on a divine oath.

The promise that God made to David is further explained in 2 Samuel 11:12–17. This promise will be fulfilled in the future after David has died. He will have a son whose kingdom will be established (7:12). This son will begin the fulfillment of the promise of an enduring dynasty and will build a house for God. The relationship between the kingdom, the temple, and this son born to David is important. One reason that David was not allowed to build the temple is because he was a man of war, fighting the Lord's battles to establish the kingdom (1 Sam. 25:28), but his son Solomon will be a man of peace. This peace, reflected in the early reign of Solomon, was the proper setting for building the temple because the temple, as the symbolical representation of the kingdom, was to correspond to the nature of that kingdom. God established David's dynasty and then allowed that dynasty to establish the Lord's temple. This connection bound David's rule to God's rule. God will maintain his permanent dwelling place as king in Israel through the kingship of the Davidic line.

Other promises that God made to David are important for understanding the Covenant with David and its role in the history of Israel (2 Sam. 7:14–16). The Davidic Covenant established a father-son relationship between God and the kings of the Davidic line (7:14). This represented a significant development in redemptive history. The king's relationship to God as son, along with his responsibilities to keep the covenant, raised the issue of the discipline of the king and what happens to the promise of a continuing dynasty if the king breaks the covenant. God specifically states that when the son commits iniquity, God will discipline him with the rod of men, but his steadfast love (*chesed*) will not be taken from him as it was taken from Saul (7:14–15). The covenant has a conditional aspect that relates to each individual king, who must keep the covenant. If the king does not keep it, God may use other nations to bring judgment against him and the people. The covenant also has an unconditional element to it so that the promises of an enduring dynasty and kingdom are not ultimately dependent on the obedience of individual kings. God will not remove his covenant loyalty from the line of David and choose another dynasty in place of it, as he did with Saul. David's dynasty, kingdom, and throne will be established forever (7:14–16). God will use the promises to David and his descendants to redeem a people for himself.

THE CULMINATION OF GOD'S COVENANT PROMISES

The promises of the Davidic Covenant bring to a culmination the previous promises that God made with his people. In this way the Davidic Covenant sets the stage for the future of God's people and the ultimate fulfillment of his promises. The idea of kingship goes back to Genesis 1:26–28 with the concept of humanity's dominion over creation. The promise of Genesis 3:15 after the Fall uses the language of warfare to describe the conflict between the seed of the woman and the seed of the serpent. The Covenant with Abraham includes the promise of kings (Gen. 15:12–16; 17:6) and the prospect of Abraham's descendants establishing dominion over the land of Canaan (Gen. 17:8). Deuteronomy 17 sets forth how this king will rule 'when you come into the land' and desire a king 'like all the nations.' Deuteronomy sets out the parameters of kingship in a theocracy where the LORD is the true king by setting limits to the rule and power of the human king. Deuteronomy 16:18–18:22 places all authority in the nation under the authority of God and his law. The law was a higher power than the word of the king (17:18–20), which kept the king from the temptations of royal power and its abuse. A balance of power among the leaders limited the power of all the offices, particularly the power of the king. The limit on horses (17:16) put a limit on the gathering of a large army because they were to trust in God for victory, not military strength. The limit of wives (17:17) limited foreign entanglements and temptations to forsaking the LORD for false gods. The limit on wealth would limit the king's accumulation of power and status above other Israelites.

As the ministry of Samuel was near its end, the elders of Israel requested 'a king to judge us like all the nations' (1 Sam. 8:5). When Samuel warned them of the dangers of kingship they responded with 'But there shall be a king over us that we also may be like all the nations, and that our king may judge us and go out before us and fight our battles' (1 Sam. 8:19–20). God told Samuel to give them a king because they had rejected God as their king (8:7, 22). Israel's first king, Saul, was a king like the nations. He was eventually rejected by God because he rejected the Word of God (1 Sam. 15). David was God's choice and through the promises of the Davidic Covenant the kingdom of God reached its zenith in the early reign of Solomon.

The Davidic Covenant did not replace the promises of the other covenants but built on them. God promised to make Abraham's name great (Gen. 12:2) and to give him descendants as numerous as the stars of heaven (Gen. 15:5) and the dust of the earth (Gen. 13:16). These promises are restated to David and are fulfilled in the early reign of Solomon. The people are as numerous as the sand by the sea (1 Kings 4:34) and the kingdom experienced peace and safety throughout the whole region (1 Kings 4:24–25). Also, the promise that all the families of the earth will be blessed (Gen. 12:3) is fulfilled as 'people of all nations came to hear the wisdom of Solomon, and from all the kings of the earth who had heard of his wisdom' (1 Kings 4:34). Several promises in the Mosaic Covenant are fulfilled in the Davidic Covenant, including the rest God granted David, the experience of covenant blessings by God's people in the land (Deut. 28:1–14; 1 Kings 4:25), and the nations witnessing God's blessings on Israel (Deut. 28:10; 1 Kings 4:30). The promise that God will be with his people (Exod. 6:6–7) is fulfilled in David (2 Sam. 7:9) and God's people (Ezek. 34:24). This promise is also fulfilled when God dwells among his people through the temple that Solomon built (1 Kings 8:54–61).

Point of Interest

The statement that the LORD 'has sought out a man after his own heart' to be king (1 Sam. 13:14) can be understood to refer to David as God's choice to be king or to David as a man who will be like-minded with the LORD and surrender to his Word. Some argue that both meanings are possible.*

---

* Robert D. Bergen, *1, 2 Samuel* (Broadman & Holman, 2002), p. 151.

THE KING AS MEDIATOR OF GOD'S PEOPLE

The Davidic dynasty is fully integrated into the religious and social dimensions of the Mosaic Covenant so that the covenant is administered by the Davidic king who takes on a prominent role in the leadership of the nation. The Davidic Covenant advances the king's position within the nation. Up to this point, Israel was God's firstborn son (Exod. 4:23), but now the king of Israel is the son with God as his Father. The special relationship of sonship means that the king serves as a mediator of the covenant. As son he shares the throne of God with his Father and has access to the Father. The special status of the king as son of God has implications for his role within Israel.

Point of Interest

When the king of Israel is considered as the son with God his Father, this should be considered as adoption of the king as son and not deification of the king. In many of the nations that surrounded Israel, the king was considered deity. In Israel, the character of God as transcendent and unique made deification of the king impossible. The prophets condemn Israelite kings for many things, but not for claiming deity for themselves.

The king was empowered to perform certain religious functions in relationship to worship. David set up the first altar for the LORD in Jerusalem and Solomon offered sacrifices at the dedication of the temple (1 Kings 8) and then at the three great feasts of the year (1 Kings 9:25). Both David and Solomon blessed the people of God in the sanctuary (2 Sam. 6:18; 1 Kings 8:14). However, this special role of the king did not mean that he was a priest or could perform all the priestly functions (2 Chron. 26:16–21). The king was the religious head of the people, but he was not a priest in the strict sense.

The special status of the king as son had implications for the role of the king in keeping the covenant. The king represented the people so that his actions of obedience or disobedience became part of the basis for whether God's people experienced his judgment or blessings. The people were still indicted for

---

Point of Interest

Passages that present the kings of Israel offering sacrifices and performing some priestly activities has led to the view that there was a royal priesthood in Israel based on the order of Melchizedek in Psalm 110.* However, the scriptural evidence for this view is too ambiguous to draw definite conclusions about a priestly order according to Melchizedek that historically existed in Israel. There was a clear division in the Old Testament between the kings and the Levitical priests in Israel which limited the actions a king could perform in the temple (2 Chron. 26:16–21). The priesthood of Melchizedek was a type of a heavenly priesthood that only Jesus could fulfill.

---

* Eugene H. Merrill, 'Royal Priesthood: An Old Testament Messianic Motif', *BSac* 150 (January-March 1993), 53.

---

their sin, and they were held responsible for the judgment of exile (Jer. 2–6), but special responsibility fell on the king to follow God and obey the law. Otherwise, he was also held responsible for God's judgment (Jer. 22; Ezek. 34).

There were also implications for Jerusalem which was the center of God's plan for the nations. The throne of God was identified as the throne of the Davidic king so that Jerusalem became the center from which God would exercise his sovereignty over the nations through the king. When Solomon built the temple, Jerusalem was established as the place of God's presence and the focal point of the religious life of God's people in worship and in looking to it for God's help in times of need (1 Kings 8). It also became the geographical location for the fulfillment of Israel's mission to the nations. The early reign of Solomon was a fulfillment of this mission as the Queen of Sheba and kings from other nations came to Jerusalem to see the great things God was doing (1 Kings 4:29–34; 10:1–13). The promises of the Davidic Covenant were fulfilled in David's son, Solomon. The early reign of Solomon brought Israel to the height of her power and influence. The sad reality is that the later disobedience of Solomon (1 Kings 11) and the kings that followed him led to the judgment of exile and the loss of kingship. But the promises of the Davidic Covenant kept the hope alive that one from the throne of David would come to rule God's people.

9

The New Covenant

The history of God's people in the Old Testament was primarily a history of disobedience. The blessings of Solomon's reign did not last because his heart was turned away from the Lord by his foreign wives (1 Kings 11:1–8). Although the kingdom of Israel divided into the northern and southern kingdoms after Solomon, God kept his promise to David by not taking the whole kingdom away from his descendants (1 Kings 11:34–36), which was represented in the dynasty that continued in the southern kingdom of Judah. God's faithfulness to his covenant promise to David was expressed in the phrase 'for the sake of my servant David' (1 Kings 11:32, 34). Sometimes the shortened phrase is used, 'for David's sake' which occurs at several points in the history of the southern kingdom. It can be used in a positive sense as a promise to Hezekiah that God will defend the city of Jerusalem (2 Kings 19:34; 20:6). It can be used in a negative sense in response to the disobedience of the kings of the southern kingdom to show that for David's sake he will not destroy Judah (2 Kings 8:19). However, the disobedience of the people and the king continued and increased to the extent that God brought the curse of the covenant in the destruction of Jerusalem and the temple in 587 B.C. All the covenant promises of God seemed to be in jeopardy. The promises of the Abrahamic Covenant of a great name, descendants as numerous as the stars of heaven, and the possession of the land were dashed as they lost their land and were taken to Babylon in exile. Israel failed in her mission to be a holy nation and a kingdom of priests to the nations by adopting the wicked ways of the nations. The fulfillment of the promise of an enduring kingdom and a descendant of David to sit on the throne was now in doubt. Such events were hardly believable to the people (Jer. 7:4) even though Jeremiah and Ezekiel had prophesied these very events. There was perhaps no lower point of Israel's history than the devastating events of 587 B.C.

WILL GOD'S PROMISES TO DAVID BE FULFILLED?

Several passages of Scripture wrestle with the implications of the apparent failure of the covenant promises to David. Of course, the failure is not found in the promises themselves, or in the God who made them, but in the disobedience of the king and people. And yet, God had committed himself to fulfill certain promises so it is natural that questions would arise in relationship to those promises, specifically the promises to David. Did the removal of the Davidic king from Jerusalem and the lack of a king to rule over God's people mean that God's promises to David had come to an end?

Psalm 89 wrestles with the question of the failure of God's covenant faithfulness. It has three sections: a hymn to the LORD for his faithfulness (89:1–18), a review of the promises of the Davidic Covenant (89:19–37), and a lament over the apparent failure of the promises to David (89:38–51). The key words of the psalm are 'steadfast love' (*chesed*) and 'faithfulness' (*emunah*). The hymn praises God's faithfulness by showing how the heavens and the heavenly hosts praise the power of God, whose rule exemplifies God's steadfast love and faithfulness. The promises of God to David display the same enduring stability as creation because the God who rules creation made an oath to David (89:3) to establish his throne (89:29). The strong statements of God's steadfast love and faithfulness to establish David's throne and that he will not violate the covenant make the lament that questions God's faithfulness even more jarring to the reader (89:38–45). But the current humiliation of the king has an explanation that goes back to the Davidic Covenant itself (2 Sam. 7:14–15). The Davidic kings have not obeyed God and his wrath has been poured out against his anointed (89:31–33, 38). The questions in verses 46–51 are a cry for God to fulfill his covenant promises to David by moving beyond discipline and wrath to show his faithfulness again to the Davidic line. The issue of God's steadfast love is raised in the question of Psalm 89:49, 'Lord, where is your steadfast love of old, which by your faithfulness you swore to David?' God has been faithful to the covenant

---

Point of Interest

The question, 'where is your steadfast love?' in Psalm 89:49 is answered in Book 4 of the Psalter (90–106). With the temple and the city of Jerusalem destroyed, Book 4 goes back to the foundations with a psalm of Moses that emphasizes the eternal nature of God and the frailty of human life. Psalm 92 affirms the continuing steadfast love of the LORD and Psalms 93–100 assert that the LORD still reigns among his people even if there is no Davidic king. Psalms of David (101, 103) and other psalms (102, 104) declare the continued blessings of God for his people and for creation. God has demonstrated his wondrous deeds in the history of Israel (Ps. 105), but God's people have at the same time continued to rebel against him, which has led to their exile (Ps. 106). Psalm 106 ends with the cry of God's people 'to save us and gather us from the nations.' This is answered in Psalm 107, the first psalm of Book V, 'let the redeemed of the LORD say so, who he has ... gathered in from the lands' (vv. 2–3).*

---

* For more on the structure of the Psalter and the meaning of Psalms 89 and 132, see Richard P. Belcher, Jr., *The Messiah of the Psalms* (Ross-shire: Christian Focus, 2006).

to bring the discipline of judgment. Will he also be faithful to show his steadfast love as he promised?

Psalm 132 is a royal psalm that promises the restoration of the Davidic king based on God's promise to David that one of his descendants would sit on the throne 'forever' (132:12). Jerusalem as God's dwelling place is also emphasized. The basic structure of the psalm highlights the parallels between David's concern to establish a dwelling place for the LORD (132:1–10) and God's covenant promises concerning David's descendants (132:11–18). God is exhorted to remember the efforts of David for the ark so that he will act on behalf of the Davidic king, the anointed one, to establish his throne (132:10–12). God promises that the strength ('horn') of David would be restored, and his dynasty would not be extinguished, but would rather shine like a lamp.

Psalms 89 and 132 give God's people hope that the Davidic dynasty will be restored. The rejection of the king in Psalm 89 is not final. Psalm 89:39 laments the defilement of the crown of the 'anointed one,' but 132:18 affirms that the crown of the 'anointed one' will shine. In Psalm 89:42 the enemies have triumphed over the king, but in 132:18 the enemies are defeated and humiliated. There is hope that a king will come, a horn will sprout for David.

THE PROMISE OF A NEW COVENANT

Hope for the restoration of God's purposes for his people is also expressed in the promise of a New Covenant. Although Jeremiah 31:31 is the only place in the Old Testament where the term 'New Covenant' is used, the concept is expressed in other passages of Scripture, particularly Ezekiel 36, along with other prophecies of restoration that also mention the covenant promises of God (Ezekiel 33–39). Although most of the book of Jeremiah is about God's judgment, chapters 30–33 are devoted to prophecies of restoration. Many other covenant promises are emphasized in these chapters of Jeremiah. The covenant formula, 'And you shall be my people and I will be your God' is mentioned twice (30:22; 31:1). The land is a key promise of Abraham and for restoration to take place the people must be brought back to their land from exile (30:4–11). God promises repentance and forgiveness (30:12–17), the repopulation of the land, a reversal of the judgment suffered by God's people (31:2–6), a rejoicing over the goodness of God and renewed blessings (31:7–14). There is also a call for God's people to respond to his mercy (31:18–22) with hope expressed for the rebuilding of Jerusalem (Jer. 33:1–13). The promise of a king in the Davidic Covenant and the implications for God's people is highlighted in Jeremiah 33:14–26. Without a king there can be no kingdom and no full restoration of the people. At some point in the future, God declares that he

> **Point of Interest**
>
> Jeremiah 33:17–18 promises that David shall never lack a man to sit on the throne and the Levitical priests shall never lack a man to offer sacrifices. The fact that the Levitical priesthood becomes obsolete in the New Covenant seems to go against what this passage promised. Christ, however, fulfills the Old Testament offices and transforms them so that they continue in greater ways. Christ now sits on the throne of David, but it is a heavenly throne at the right hand of the Father. Christ transforms the temple and the priesthood so that the ministry of the church, the new temple of God, is carried out by the sacrifices of his people. This fulfills Isaiah 66:21 that Gentiles can serve as priests and Levites.

will fulfill the promise that someone from the Davidic line will be raised up to execute righteousness in the land and to save his people (33:14–16).

The certainty of these promises is reinforced by a reference to the stability of the day and night, 'my covenant with the day and my covenant with the night' (33:20) and 'the fixed order of heaven and earth' (33:25). Although this could be a reference to creation, many take it to be a reference to the Noahic Covenant.* In other words, if anyone can break the terms of the Noahic Covenant so that day and night do not come at their appointed time, then the covenant with David and the Levites can be broken (33:20-21). This is an impossible scenario meant to demonstrate that even though it appears God's covenant promises are in jeopardy, God will fulfill them.

The promise of a New Covenant (31:31-34) is given in the context of the assurance of the fulfillment of other covenant promises, including return to the land, the rebuilding of Jerusalem, and promises made to Abraham, Levi, and David. There are also promises of healing, forgiveness, joy, and prosperity. The promise of the New Covenant seems to be the central promise of Jeremiah 30-33 so that the fulfillment of the other covenant promises will be dependent on the fulfillment of the promises of the New Covenant. The promises in Jeremiah 31:31-34 focus on the spiritual relationship between God and his people. This covenant is made with the houses of Israel and Judah in the coming days. At some point in the future the LORD will act to restore the fortunes of his reunited people. The New Covenant will not be like the Mosaic Covenant which the people broke by their disobedience. God then declares the character of the New Covenant by laying out what it will accomplish in the lives of the people:

(1) 'I will put my law within them, and I will write it on their hearts'
(2) 'I will be their God and they shall be my people'

---

* John L. MacKay, *Jeremiah Vol. 2: Chapters 21-53* (Christian Focus, 2004), p. 281.

(3) 'they shall all know me, from the least to the greatest'

(4) 'I will forgive their iniquity, and I will remember their sin no more'

These promises were also part of the purpose of the Mosaic Covenant (Deut. 6:5–6; Exod. 6:7; Deut. 4:35; Lev. 1:4; 4:27–31). The Mosaic Covenant partook of the provisional, shadowy nature of the types and ordinances (sacrifices, circumcision, the paschal lamb) found in the Old Testament that pointed to the coming of the Messiah. Moses had no power as mediator of the covenant to bring about its fulfillment, but Christ as the mediator of the New Covenant would have the power to establish it in the lives of God's people (Heb. 8:1–6). The author of Hebrews quotes the full passage from Jeremiah 31:31–34 (8:8–12) to show the need of the New Covenant to bring to fruition those promises, which also makes the first covenant obsolete (8:13).

> **Point of Interest**
>
> One should not conclude that there were not any true believers in the Old Testament. Abraham was justified by faith (Gen. 15:6) and the language of sanctification is used of David in Psalm 51. Although the Old Testament institutions were types and shadows of a coming reality, they were sufficient to communicate God's grace to his people, looking forward to the day that Christ would come (WCF 7.5).

The promises of the New Covenant take on the provisional nature of the kingdom that Christ established in line with Paul's statement that we have only received a down payment on our full inheritance (Eph. 1:13–14). The promise that God will write his law on the hearts of his people has already begun in the lives of believers, but it is not yet completed because obedience is not yet perfected in God's people. Battling the old nature is still part of the believer's experience (Gal. 5:16–26).

The essence of the covenant relationship ('I will be their God and they shall be my people') is also a present reality. Although this covenant relationship cannot be broken for those who are true believers, they still need to be disciplined by God to keep them from straying (Heb. 12:3–17). The forgiveness of sins is a reality in the lives of believers, but sin continues to be a problem so that repentance is a constant need to take care of ongoing sin. The promise that 'they shall all know me, from the least of them to the greatest' also takes on the provisional nature of the 'now, but not yet character' of life in the church before the second coming of Christ. There is a legal sense to the administration of the covenant whereby someone can be part of the covenant legally but not have a saving relationship with God through Christ (the personal aspect of the covenant). This would refer to someone who has made a profession of faith that turns out to be false, or someone who has been baptized as an infant. Such individuals are part of the new covenant community and receive the appropriate benefits relative to their situation that come from being part of the corporate body of believers.

The legal aspect of the administration of the covenant is affirmed by several passages of Scripture. In Romans 11:16–24 Paul affirms the unity between Israel and the church by means of an olive tree. The branches of the olive tree are holy by virtue of being connected to the root of the tree, which is also holy. But some of the branches were broken off because of unbelief (v. 20). Paul then warns the Gentiles, who are part of the New Covenant, that the same thing could happen to them (vv. 21–22). They too are considered part of the olive tree, and are thus holy, but they can also be cut off from the tree because of unbelief. If someone falls away because of unbelief it shows that they did not have a saving relationship with God. Not everyone who is part of the New Covenant community is a true believer. Not every confession of faith is a true confession. The visible church may have people who are members but who are not true believers. The book of Hebrews issues warnings to its members not to drift away (2:1–4) and not to fall away with an unbelieving heart (3:12), lest there be grave consequences (6:1–7). Such consequences could include church discipline (1 Cor. 5:1). The invisible church, however, is only composed of the elect who will not break the covenant through unbelief. In the new heavens and new earth God's people will experience perfected natures that no longer need to be exhorted to holiness because they will no longer struggle with sin. Christ's second coming is truly our 'blessed hope' (Titus 2:12–13).

10

Christ Fulfills All Covenant Promises

Each of the covenants have their distinctive promises that are developed in redemptive history and are fulfilled in Jesus Christ. In the initiation of the Covenant of Grace in Genesis 3:15, God promised that the seed of the woman would crush the head of the serpent. The godly line developed through the line of Seth, but wickedness increased on the earth until God decided to destroy the world by a flood. Noah, who found favor with God, and his family are preserved by God in the ark. After the flood, God established a covenant with Noah and all creation, promising to preserve the created order so redemptive history could move forward. Noah was a second Adam who continued the mandate given to Adam amid a fallen world. Sin was still a problem as seen in the drunkenness of Noah and the Tower of Babel. In response to the increase of sin, God began to work out his purposes for the salvation of the world through one man and his family. He called Abram to go to a land that he would show him, promising to give to him and his descendants the land of Canaan, to make his name great, and to make him a blessing to the nations. God committed himself to fulfill these promises in the covenant of Genesis 15, including the promise to make Abraham's descendants as numerous as the stars of heaven

(15:5). God's commitment to Abraham's descendants (seed) is further confirmed in the sign of circumcision (17:9–14) with the promise 'to be God to you and your offspring after you' (17:7). God changed Abram's name to Abraham to show that he will be a father of many nations with kings coming from him (17:6).

The full promise of kingship related to a descendant of Abraham awaited further developments, but God promised that the scepter would be associated with the tribe of Judah (49:8–12) and that a ruler would arise to crush the enemies of God's people (Num. 24:17–18). Regulations related to the king were given in Deuteronomy 17:14–20 'when you come into the land.' These regulations were part of the Mosaic Covenant where Israel was made into a nation, given a law, and a mission focused on the land of Canaan. The Mosaic Covenant was foundational for the development of kingship and for understanding the history of Israel and her loss of the land in exile, which was related to the blessings and curses of the covenant (Deut. 27–28). God's covenant commitment to the dynasty of David was expressed in 2 Samuel 7, but those promises seemed in jeopardy in the destruction of Jerusalem, the temple, and the monarchy in 587 B.C. (Ps. 89:38–51). The promises of each covenant revolved around Israel existing as a nation in the land God had given to her. The loss of king, nation, and land made it difficult to see how those promises could ever be fulfilled.

God told Israel through Isaiah the prophet that he was able to fulfill his promises by bringing the people back to their land. He would raise up Cyrus, king of Persia, who defeated Babylon in 539 B.C. and issued a decree in 538 B.C. that Israel could return to her land. Those who returned to the land began the slow process of trying to reconstitute themselves as a nation even while being under the control of Persia. Conditions were difficult. They cleared rubble from the temple site and built an altar but got caught up in trying to establish their own lives and built their own houses (Haggai 1:2–6). God raised up two prophets, Haggai and Zechariah, to get the people to rebuild the temple which was dedicated in 516 B.C. Ezra the scribe returned to Judah to help in the restoration by focusing on the Mosaic Covenant with an emphasis on law, purity, and separation. Nehemiah became governor of Judah and rebuilt the wall of Jerusalem. By 400 B.C. many Israelites had returned to their land, the temple was operating, the walls of Jerusalem had been built, and attempts had been made to live by the Mosaic Covenant. Israel was trying to become a nation, with a law, living in the land given to them by God. But there were major problems in the post-exilic community. The book of Malachi shows that the people were not faithful in their relationships with each other, and the priests were allowing the people to bring blemished animals to sacrifice against the regulations of the Mosaic Covenant. Israel was in the land and had the law, but they were not fulfilling their mission to the nations and were lacking a king to sit on the throne according to the promise of the Davidic Covenant. The scene was set for a king to come to fulfill God's covenant promises.

THE NATURE OF CHRIST'S KINGDOM

It is significant that Jesus came proclaiming, 'The time is fulfilled, and the kingdom of God is at hand; repent and believe in the gospel' (Mark 1:15; see also Matt. 4:17). The king has come to establish his kingdom. The nature of this kingdom is very important for understanding the fulfillment of God's covenant promises.

The people of Jesus' day were expecting a king like David to destroy their enemies and establish Israel as a great nation. They were expecting a powerful king who would establish a powerful, political kingdom, a territory or realm over which the king would rule. This expectation is encouraged by the fact that Jesus is of the line of David. He is called the son of David (Matt. 1:1; 12:23), the king of the Jews (Matt. 2:2), the Messiah (Christ) who fulfills Old Testament prophecies (Matt. 2:4–6), and the beloved Son in whom God is well pleased (Matt. 3:16). Mary is told by the angel that the son she will bear will be 'called the Son of the Most High' and 'the Lord will give him the throne of his father David, and he will reign over the house of Jacob forever, and of his kingdom there will be no end' (Luke 1:31–33).

The evidence of Jesus' kingship is seen in his power to rule creation (Matt. 8:23–27; Mark 4:35–41; Luke 8:24), his healing people of illness and disease (Matt. 4:25; Mark 1:29–33), and his power over the spiritual forces of wickedness in casting out demons (Mark 1:21–28; Luke 4:31–37). He also demonstrated power over life and death by raising people from the dead (Matt. 9:22–26; Mark 5:35–43; Luke 8:49–58).

Jesus did not meet the expectations of the people for a king who would lead Israel into a revolt against the Roman government. In other words, they did not understand the nature of his kingdom. Jesus came to establish a spiritual kingdom that could be entered immediately by submitting to the rule of Jesus through faith in him. The word kingdom can refer to the authority of a king to exercise rule and all those who believe in Jesus submit their lives to his rule. The kingdom that Jesus came to establish was also a spiritual kingdom as he healed a paralytic to show his power to forgive sins (Mark 2:1–12). He overcame Satan's temptations (Matt. 4:1–11) and did battle with the demons (Matt. 12:22–32). Jesus defined his kingdom as operating differently than the kingdoms of the world by bearing witness to the truth (18:36–37). The present, spiritual reality of the kingdom meant, according to the parables, that the kingdom begins small, is hidden in the way it works, and can be rejected by people. Yet Christ now reigns as king. He sits at the right hand of the Father governing the world for the sake of his people (Eph. 1:22). The promises of the Davidic Covenant are fulfilled in Christ who is the descendant of David, the son who occupies the throne of David. He is the horn who sprouted for David (see also Ezek. 29:21, Luke 1:69) and the highest of the kings of the earth as the firstborn of creation (Ps. 89:27; Col. 1:15), both son of David and Son of God (Rom. 1:3–4). Jesus fulfilled the conditions of the covenant by keeping the law perfectly and bearing in himself the chastening judgments deserved by David's descendants through their covenant violations (Ps. 89:38–45). God was faithful to his covenant promises to David and those who believe in Jesus Christ are the beneficiaries of the rest, salvation, and security that results from believing in Jesus as the Son of God and the savior of his people.

The fullness of Christ's kingdom, however, has not yet come. The manifestation of Christ as king to the world awaits his future coming when Jesus will appear in glory at the end of the age, the enemies of God will be defeated, and God's people will receive the fullness of their inheritance. Christ will reign not only in the hearts of his people, but also over the whole world (Rev. 11:15). This kingdom comes by the power of God, not by wisdom or human effort. The present, spiritual reality of Christ's kingdom is important for understanding the fulfillment of the Old Testament. The promises of the Old Testament are fulfilled now for God's people in a provisional way and will be fulfilled in a complete way in the future when Jesus comes to establish the fullness of his reign. Then we will experience the fullness of salvation in the new heavens and earth.

THE CONSUMMATION OF THE COVENANT PROMISES

The land promise is central to the covenant promises of the Old Testament. God called Abram to leave his father's house and go

---

Point of Interest

With the fulfillment of the Old Testament covenant promises in Jesus Christ certain changes take place related to the existence of God's people and their mission. No longer is there a commitment to one geographical location but the mission encompasses the whole world. No longer are God's people constituted a nation with a civil government but now God's people are a spiritual people scattered among many nations. The church is not dependent on physical warfare to accomplish its purposes but advances its cause through spiritual warfare focused on proclaiming the good news of the gospel. These changes hinge on the nature of the kingdom that Christ came to establish.

---

to the land he would show him with the promise that he would give it to his descendants. The land is the place where the other covenant promises of God would be fulfilled and where Israel would fulfill her mission to the nations as a kingdom of priests and a holy nation. The nations would come to Israel to learn about the goodness of God and the great law that he had given to his people. Although this mission was partially fulfilled under Solomon's reign, Solomon turned away from the Lord and the kingdom divided. The Servant Songs of Isaiah (49:1–5; 52:13–53:12) show that even though Israel failed in her mission, God raised up another Servant who would succeed in bringing Israel back to God and in ministering to the nations. Jesus is that servant who shows that the place where one worships is no longer important. Rather, the Father seeks those who will worship in spirit and in truth (John 4:23–24). Focus on land as a specific geographic location is expanded considering the mission the resurrected Christ gives to his people to go into all the world. The good news of the message of the gospel is to be taken to every nation. Abraham was heir of the land but in the New Covenant he is the heir of the world (Rom. 4:13). The inheritance of the followers of Christ is the world, but we have not yet fully received that inheritance. Christ now rules the world, including all the nations, and our mission as his people is to bring the good news of the gospel to the nations in anticipation of Jesus' coming again where we will inherit the new heavens and new earth.

In the new heavens and the new earth all the covenant promises of God will be completely fulfilled. The promise of a people (the seed promise) reaches its fulfillment when God's people worship him (Rev. 22:3; 7:15) and see his face (22:3).

Point of Interest

The book of Hebrews makes the point that God's people in the Old Testament were looking for more than an earthly fulfillment of the promises that God had made to them. According to Hebrews 11:13–16, the faith of Old Testament believers was forward-looking because they did not view this world as their real home but 'acknowledged that they were strangers and exiles on the earth' (v. 13). They were seeking something beyond the earthly promise of a homeland to a better heavenly country, a city prepared by God (vv. 14–16). Abraham himself understood that the land was a shadow of a final dwelling place. Hebrews does not cancel out the promises made in the Old Testament, but these promises are fulfilled in Christ in a way that brings about a greater reality of those promises in the ministry of Christ and in the dwelling of God with his people.

The radiance of God and the Lamb will be so bright that there will be no need of the sun (22:5) or a temple for the Lord God Almighty and the Lamb will be the temple (21:22). The promise of God's dwelling with his people is fully realized as he will dwell with them and they shall be his people (21:3). The promise of worldwide blessing given to Abraham is fulfilled as the nations come for healing (22:2). There is no sin, impurity, or curse in this city as God's people are perfected by the power of God (21:27; 22:3, 14–15). Thus, there is no pain, mourning, or death (21:4) and no need for the forgiveness of sin for God's people will be perfect, not able to sin and able to keep the law. We should live today in the light of this glorious destiny. As the hymn states it, 'and the things of this earth will grow strangely dim in the light of his glory and grace.'* Even so, come quickly Lord Jesus, amen!

---

* From the hymn 'Turn Your Eyes Upon Jesus' in the Trinity Hymnal (Great Commissions Publications, 1990).

Suggested Reading

The following list is very selective. Some approaches, such as Federal Vision, are not listed. For interaction and evaluation of Federal Vision and many of the views listed below see Belcher, *The Fulfillment of the Promises of God*.

TRADITIONAL WCF VIEW OF COVENANT THEOLOGY

Belcher, Jr., Richard P. *The Fulfillment of the Promises of God: An Explanation of Covenant Theology*. Ross-shire: Christian Focus, 2020.

Fesko, J.V. *The Trinity and the Covenant of Redemption*. Ross-shire: Christian Focus, 2016.

_____. *Adam and the Covenant of Works*. Ross-shire: Christian Focus, 2021.

Meyers, Stephen G. *God to Us: Covenant Theology in Scripture*. Grand Rapids: Reformation Heritage Books, 2021.

Rhodes, Jonty. *Covenants Made Simple: Understanding God's Unfolding Promises to His People*. Phillipsburg, NJ: P&R, 2013.

Waters, Guy P., J. Nicholas Reid, and John R. Muether, eds. *Covenant Theology: Biblical, Theological, and Historical Perspectives*. Wheaton: Crossway, 2020.

MINOR VARIATIONS FROM WCF VIEW OF COVENANT THEOLOGY

Murray, John. *The Covenant of Grace*. Phillipsburg, NJ: P&R Publishing, 1953.

> Murray denies a Covenant of Works but has many of the elements of the Covenant of Works in his Adamic Administration. He has a solid view of justification by faith and imputation.

————. 'The Adamic Administration' (pp. 47–59 in the *Collected Writings of John Murray: Volume Two, Select Lectures in Systematic Theology*. Carlisle, PA: The Banner of Truth Trust, 1977).

Robertson, O. Palmer. *The Christ of the Covenants*. Phillipsburg, NJ: P&R Publishing, 1980.

> Robertson's work is a classic that is beneficial to read. He does not always use the terminology of the WCF in his descriptions of covenant theology.

MEREDITH KLINE'S VIEW OF COVENANT THEOLOGY

Kline is fascinating to read and helpful in many areas. He also has some distinctive views of Covenant Theology. The following works, except one, are supportive of Kline's views.

Brown, Michael G. and Zach Keele. *Sacred Bond: Covenant Theology Explored*. Grandville, MI: Reformed Fellowship, Inc., 2012.

Elam, Andrew M, Robert C. Van Kooten, and Randall A. Bergquist. *Moses and Merit: A Critique of the Klinean Doctrine of Republication*. Eugene, OR: Wipf & Stock, 2014.

Estelle, Bryan D., J. V. Fesko, and David VanDrunen. *The Law is Not of Faith: Essays on Works and Grace in the Mosaic Covenant*. Phillipsburg, NJ: P&R Publishing, 2009.

Horton, Michael. *God of Promise: Introducing Covenant Theology*. Grand Rapids: Baker Books, 2006.

Kline, Meredith. *Kingdom Prologue: Genesis Foundations for a Covenantal Worldview*. Eugene, OR: Wipf & Stock, 2006.

————. *Treaty of the Great King: The Covenant Structure of Deuteronomy*. Eugene, OR: Wipf & Stock, 2012.

CONFESSIONAL BAPTISTS

Barcellos, Richard C., ed. *Recovering a Covenantal Heritage: Essays in Baptist Covenant Theology*. Palmdale, CA: RBAP, 2014.

Blackburn, Earl M., ed. *Covenant Theology: A Baptist Distinctive*. Birmingham, AL: Solid Ground Christian Books, 2013.

Griffiths, Phillip D. R. *Covenant Theology: A Reformed Baptist Perspective*. Eugene, OR: Wipf & Stock, 2016.

Johnson, Jeffrey D. *The Kingdom of God: A Baptist Expression of Covenant and Biblical Theology*. Conway AR: Free Grace Press, 2014.

Renihan, James M., ed. *Covenant Theology: From Adam to Christ*. Palmdale, CA: Reformed Baptist Academic Press, 2005.

Renihan, Samuel. *The Mystery of Christ: His Covenant and His Kingdom*. Cape Coral, FL: Founders Press, 2019.

EVANGELICAL AND OTHER BAPTIST VIEWS

Gentry, Peter J. and Stephen J. Wellum. *Kingdom Through Covenant: A Biblical-Theological Understanding of the Covenants*. Wheaton: Crossway, 2018.

Schriener, Thomas R. *Covenant and God's Purpose for the World*. Wheaton: Crossway, 2017.

Wellum, Stephen J., and Brent E. Parker, eds. *Progressive Covenantalism*. Nashville, TN: B&H Academic, 2016.

Williamson, Paul R. *Sealed with an Oath: Covenant in God's Unfolding Purpose*. Downers Grove, IL: Inter-Varsity Press, 2007.

Also available from

Christian Focus Publications

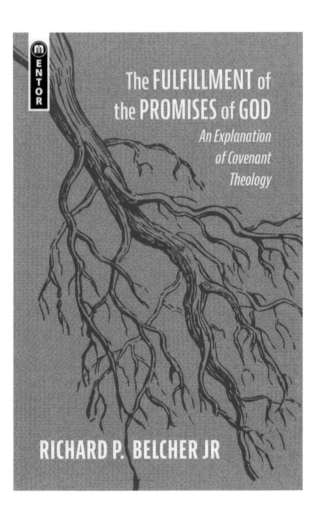

The **FULFILLMENT** of
the **PROMISES** of **GOD**

*An Explanation
of Covenant
Theology*

RICHARD P. BELCHER JR

The Fulfillment of the Promises of God
An Exploration of Covenant Theology

by Richard P. Belcher, Jr.

978-1-5271-0519-5

A variety of views and nuances of covenant theology exist within the Reformed church and the broader evangelical world. This book seeks to explain covenant theology as presented in the Westminster Confession of Faith as a starting point for discussions of covenant theology and as a foundation to evaluate other views. Some variations of covenant theology are minor and do not impact the system of doctrine of Reformed theology, but other variations are major and impact important doctrines associated with justification by faith. Attention is also given to the views of confessional Baptists, as well as those who are evangelicals and operate with a covenantal approach to Scripture. This book combines a straightforward explanation of basic covenant theology followed by more detailed analysis of other views.

THE
MESSIAH
AND THE
PSALMS

Preaching Christ from all the Psalms

RICHARD P. BELCHER JR.

The Messiah and the Psalms
Preaching Christ from all the Psalms

by Richard P. Belcher, Jr.

978-1-8455-0074-0

What is the relevance and significance of the psalms both to the New Testament and to our lives in the twenty-first century? Richard Belcher helps you understand how all the psalms relate to Christ. Some have a direct relationship, but with others the link is not so evident. He carefully explains the biblical basis for his view and then how it works with different types of psalms.

Christian Focus Publications

Our mission statement –

STAYING FAITHFUL
In dependence upon God we seek to impact the world through
literature faithful to His infallible Word, the Bible. Our aim is to ensure
that the Lord Jesus Christ is presented as the only hope to obtain
forgiveness of sin, live a useful life and look forward to heaven with
Him.

Our Books are published in four imprints:

CHRISTIAN
FOCUS

popular works including biographies,
commentaries, basic doctrine and
Christian living.

CHRISTIAN
HERITAGE

books representing some of the best
material from the rich heritage of the
church.

MENTOR

books written at a level suitable for
Bible College and seminary students,
pastors, and other serious readers. The
imprint includes commentaries,
doctrinal studies, examination of
current issues and church history.

CF4•K

children's books for quality Bible
teaching and for all age groups:
Sunday school curriculum, puzzle and
activity books; personal and family
devotional titles, biographies and
inspirational stories – because you are
never too young to know Jesus!

Christian Focus Publications Ltd,
Geanies House, Fearn, Ross-shire,
IV20 1TW, Scotland, United Kingdom.
www.christianfocus.com